Praying
with FIRE

Seeking His Presence through the
Revival Passages of Scripture

Mark D. Partin, D.Min.

PRAYERSHOP
PUBLISHING

Terre Haute, Indiana

PrayerShop Publishing is the publishing arm of Harvest Prayer Ministries and the Church Prayer Leaders Network. Harvest Prayer Ministries exists to make every church a house of prayer.

Its online prayer store, www.prayershop.org, has more than 400 prayer resources available for purchase.

Sources for Greek translations come from Marvin R. Vincent, *Vincent's Word Studies of the New Testament*, vol.1–4.

ISBN: 978-1-935012-45-0

1 2 3 4 5 | 2017 2016 2015 2014 2013

Contents

Preface

A revival happens when almighty God pours out His presence on His people. He ministers conviction, holiness, cleansing, restoration, and empowerment to His people so that He can use them. When God blows His breath into a person or church and gives a fresh awareness and anointing of His presence and Holy Spirit, a revival occurs. In his book *Ablaze with His Glory,* Del Fehsenfeld Jr. explains revival this way:

> Revival is all about God's glory in the church! (Ephesians 3:20). When God's glory convicts, cleanses, fills and empowers our churches, then the light of Christ radiating through us will penetrate the darkness of this lost world. When we stop pretending that things are all right and begin to cry out to God for mercy, only then can we expect a visitation from God.
>
> Revival, no matter how great or how small in its ultimate scope, always begins with individual believers whose hearts are desperate for God and who are willing to pay the price to meet with Him... Let Him begin His refreshing, reviving work in you!
>
> There is no human solution that can remedy our spiritual condition, but there stands ready and waiting a Great Physician, risen with healing in His wings. He will surely come to us when we seek Him with all our hearts.[1]

If there ever was a time that the people of God needed revival, it is now. Revival can come to you personally and it can come on a corporate level. Be warned, however, that the goal is not revival for revival's sake. The goal is always to seek the Great Reviver. Praying Scripture is the surest way to pray in the will of God about all things in addition to revival. May God continue to open our eyes to the tremendous truths about revival in His Word.

How to Use This Book

This book can be used by individuals or groups. Each chapter provides a Scripture passage about revival and explains a principle found in that revival. Those who want to dig deeper can look up the additional listed references. Heartfelt prayers for revival based on the Scripture follow and may be best used individually. If you are leading a group study, you may want to allow a period of quiet so that participants will be encouraged to use the prayers at that time.

Reflection questions at the end of each chapter prompt readers to examine their lives in light of each revival principle. In a group situation, since many of the questions require vulnerability, you may want to model that quality by volunteering your answers first. Don't be afraid to allow silence. Most questions require honest introspection and may be just the tool God will use to spark revival in you and among your group.

Introduction

REVIVAL: Our Greatest Need

Revival begins in the heart of one.
Wilburn Smith, *The Glorious Revival under Hezekiah*

SCRIPTURE:
HABAKKUK 3:2

O Lord, I have heard Your speech and was afraid; O Lord, revive Your work in the midst of the years! In the years make it known; In wrath remember mercy.

Desiring More of God

Has there ever been a time in your life that you wanted more of God; yet you did not know how to move in that area? Has there ever been a time in your life, or the life of your church family, that you desired more from God, but you did not know what to do to see this happen? I have been in that situation on more than one occasion. I know many others who have been there as well. The question is: What do you do when you don't know what to do? The answer comes by knowing what you specifically desire.

The thing I desire when I want more of God is simply this: I long for the presence of God to be real and manifest in my life. I desire a conscious awareness of God moving in my life and in my church. I desire to hear God speaking and giving me revelation, insight, and understanding. I desire God. In those times, I have asked God for revival and prayed for Him to release the wind of His Holy Spirit to blow fresh on me. Revival really does begin in one person, and then it can spread its wings and fly throughout an entire church and community to the glory of God. It always starts with one. One who will cry out. One who will respond in obedience. One who will wait upon the Lord. Oh, the power of one.

God Responds

In the fall of 2006, the church where I was pastor was blessed by a mighty movement of God. We met initially every day for forty days; yet the revival continued for eleven months. This touch from God did not just happen. Spiritual preparedness is essential to any revival, or any experience that we might hope to have with God. God seeks those who have a pure heart and clean hands. We must be willing to get right, inside and out. By harboring sin, we place ourselves in a dark room where we continue to stumble over obstacles although we desperately seek direction and light. Therefore, it is critical for us, as the body of Christ, to come together for the purpose of seeking the face of God and dealing with corporate sins, both past and present. My church had times of public confession of sin and corporate confession of sin.

Corporate confession of sin is the personal identification with, and ownership of, the sins of a group. Joel 1:14 shows us the example: "Consecrate a fast, call a sacred assembly; Gather the elders *And* all the inhabitants of the land *Into* the house of the LORD your God, And cry out to the LORD." From this verse and the passage that follows in Joel 2:12–17, we grasp the urgency and importance of corporate confession.

For my church, Indiana Avenue Church, we confessed our corporate sins. We met together on three occasions for a time of solemn assembly: a Wednesday night, a Sunday morning, and a Sunday night. The sins that were confessed and repented of were pride, lack of reverence for God and His House, prayerlessness, lack of commitment, gossip, and superficiality with one another and God.

During these solemn assemblies, we became more aligned with God in preparation for revival. The amazing thing was that after many heart-wrenching confessions and the cleansing God poured out on us, we experienced conviction that led to deeper levels of confession. During corporate confession time, many individuals confessed personal sin and God forgave and cleansed them, too. The depth of conviction moved so mightily during this revival that God revealed long-buried sin to many, and more confessions came forth.

We never asked anyone to confess publicly, but God moved individuals to confess to all. One man said, "If I am ever to be right with God, I have to confess my sin before this church." People confessed terrible, shameful sins. Some decades old. Regardless, God forgave, cleansed, and restored people right before our eyes. It all began with the obedience of one.

Revival Principles

During that time of revival, and in other seasons of prayer, God began to reveal to me principles of true revival and how they relate to the revivals in the Bible. In his book *Revive Us Again*, Walter C. Kaiser Jr. references sixteen biblical revivals. Ernest Baker, in his book *The Revivals of the Bible*, lists eighteen revivals. Combining these two lists, I find nineteen revivals in the Bible, and I added two additional revival principles found in Scripture.

My list of principles is by no means exhaustive. Each chapter explains a certain principle found in a biblical revival and prompts you to examine your life in light of that principle. Although you will find multiple principles in many revivals, I have chosen to concentrate on only one principle in each revival. Along with the revival principles, I also focus on prayer and using Scripture as the basis for prayers of revival. I hope you will use the scriptural prayers I have included in each chapter and that you will go beyond these prayers and see what God is birthing in your heart. Be aware, God uses repetition to reinforce truth.

How to Pray Scripture

Praying Scripture is praying God's Word. Hebrews 4:12 says, "For the Word of God *is* living and powerful, and sharper than any two-edged sword." When we speak and pray Scripture, we are coming into agreement with God, and His power is released to answer our prayers.

How do we pray Scripture? Before you pray, it is important that you read the context of the passage. To determine the context, take time to read the verses before and after the passage you want to use as a basis of prayer. Mull them in your mind, so you understand them.

Once you grasp the context, then begin reading or reciting God's Word in a spirit of prayer. Let the meaning of the verses become your prayer as they consume your thoughts. As you read a sentence or a phrase, pause to meditate, pray, or praise. Understand there is a direct connection between the degree to which our minds are shaped by Scripture and the degree to which our prayers are answered. John 15:7 says, "If you abide in Me, and My words abide in you, you will ask what you desire, and it shall be done for you."

First John 5:14 says, "Now this is the confidence that we have in

Him, that if we ask anything according to His will, He hears us." Not only does God hear our prayers, but He also promises to answer us when we pray in line with His will. He hastens to perform His Word. You can never be closer to praying in God's will than when you pray Scripture.

Rodney "Gypsy" Smith, a British evangelist in the late 1800s and early 1900s, was once asked how to start a revival. He answered, "Go home, lock yourself in your room and kneel down in the middle of the floor. Draw a chalk mark around yourself and ask God to start the revival inside that chalk mark. When He answers your prayer, the revival will be on."[2] Oh, that we would each draw the circle on the floor and step inside.

Scriptural Prayer for Revival

Father, in the midst of the years will You not revive Your work? Oh, Father, in the midst of my life will You revive me? Show me how to seek You. Teach my heart to melt before You. Pierce my soul that I may align my life to You. Father, in the midst of busyness and business as usual, revive me. In the name of Jesus, amen.

Chapter 1

REVIVAL under JACOB: Hearing God

When Moses saw it, he marveled at the sight; as he drew near to observe, the voice of the Lord came to him, saying, "I am the God of your fathers—the God of Abraham, the God of Isaac, and the God of Jacob." And Moses trembled and dared not look. (ACTS 7:31–32)

SCRIPTURE:
GENESIS 35:1–3, 7

Then God said to Jacob, "Arise, go up to Bethel and dwell there; and make an altar there to God, who appeared to you when you fled from the face of Esau your brother."

And Jacob said to his household and to all who *were* with him, "Put away the foreign Gods that *are* among you, purify yourselves, and change your garments. Then let us arise and go up to Bethel; and I will make an altar there to God, who answered me in the day of my distress and has been with me in the way which I have gone.". . .

And he built an altar there and called the place El Bethel, because there God appeared to him when he fled from the face of his brother.

Hearing God Speak

How is your hearing? Maybe I should ask: How are your listening skills? Let's further refine the question: How are your spiritual listening skills?

The story is told of a farmer visiting his cousin in the big city. The farmer stopped in the middle of the busy sidewalk with all the hustle and bustle and said to his cousin, "Do you hear the cricket?"

The city cousin replied, "No. How can you hear a cricket in the midst of all the noise? The squealing brakes, the horns blowing, people talking, laughing, sirens blaring?"

The farmer replied, "You hear what you are used to hearing."

We hear what we are used to hearing. Are you accustomed to hearing God speak to you? God, our heavenly Father, communicates. He speaks. He initiates conversation. To be able to hear God is crucial for our spiritual lives and for revival. God speaks, and we are responsible to listen and hear Him. There are always four voices competing for our attention: the voice of God, the devil, others, and our own. We must discern which is which. By faith, we can hear God and distinguish His voice. By faith, we can receive God's Word. By faith, the children of God are enabled to hear divine truth and convert that truth to action.

God speaks in several ways today. He speaks primarily through the Bible. The Holy Spirit speaks to us by impressing God's Word and God's will upon our hearts and minds. God also speaks through godly ministers and speakers, such as pastors, preachers, teachers, and evangelists. God even speaks through our circumstances.

Responding to Truth

Regardless of the method, when God speaks He expects a response from us. He expects us to hear His voice, adjust our lives to Him, and obey. In times of revival, God speaks clearly and compellingly, and we must obey His Word quickly. When God speaks to a person, that person has encountered truth. Jesus tells us in John 14:6 that He is "the way, the truth and the life." Jesus Christ is truth. In any encounter with truth, we encounter God. And an encounter with God requires a response.

When God spoke to Jacob in Genesis 35, it was thirty years after he had experienced salvation while fleeing from his brother Esau (Genesis 28). Jacob had twenty years of fear before facing up to Esau and reconciling with him. Fear of man is the biblical term for insecurity. It took Jacob ten more years to return to Bethel—the place God instructed him to go—for full restoration.

Why did Jacob wait so long? The same reason you and I fail to respond quickly to God—pride. Pride keeps us content as we are. Pride blinds us to our true spiritual condition. When we have pride and God says something we do not agree with, we ignore it. Pride keeps us from responding to God as we should. It keeps us from personal and corporate revival.

Thankfully, in God's grace, He still speaks to us. He speaks louder than our pride, calling us to Himself. We must respond to God's voice when He speaks. We must deal with our pride and sin, or we will not know personal or corporate revival.

Getting Personal

Our God is an initiating God. One February, I was working on a series of messages for my church. As I studied, prayed, and prepared,

God impressed on my spirit that I would preach these messages in a specific church in Florida. I was surprised, yet excited. The church in Florida had not contacted me about a revival meeting. I told no one except my secretary what God had said to me. In May of that year, I received a call from this church's pastor, asking me to hold a series of revival meetings in his church that October. I readily said, "Yes, God has already spoken to me about that."

When I spoke in that Florida church, God moved in our midst in a mighty way. His presence was manifested everywhere. Conviction of sin was strong. People acknowledged their sins and asked for forgiveness from God and others. The altar was saturated with prayers and tears every night. Services lasted four to five hours. People met throughout the day to pray and seek God, and the meetings were extended by several more days. Religious men and women were changed into men and women of God and faith. People were saved. Lives were transformed.

On Thursday morning of that week, God woke me at five a.m., and I heard Him speak. I did not hear an audible voice, but I heard His voice in my soul, heart, and mind. God said, "Your ministry will transition." I cried, praising God and thanking Him. The God of all eternity had just spoken a specific word to me. Hallelujah! I did not know what it fully meant, but I knew God had spoken to me and I would obey.

Why did God speak to me at that time and place? Partly because of the tremendous cleansing that was taking place in my life and the lives of others. The Holy Spirit peeled back layers of past sin, failures, and hurts. My pride was exposed: pride of ability and pride of accomplishment. God hates pride. I confessed my wrong attitudes. As I did, forgiveness and cleansing came. Barriers of sin were removed, barriers of doubt and unbelief. Times of refreshing came. The joy of my salvation returned. I was available and able to hear God with more clarity. It was as if my entire being was now sensitive to His voice.

How could I hear God so clearly? To begin, I was studying the Word of God. That is the primary way God speaks. Before the revival started, I had fasted seven days and sought the Lord earnestly. During the meetings, God poured out His presence strongly. So God's voice came to me as a result of my abiding in His presence. I was in a position to hear because I was earnestly seeking God, and I was in the place to hear: the place of prayer and the Word, the place of abiding.

Impressions can be confusing, since anyone can claim anything is from God. Time, however, will prove all things. Nothing that I heard God speak to me in my spirit was a doctrinal controversy. It was simply God telling me what was going to happen in my life. When God told me my ministry would transition, I told only my wife and three close friends. Soon God began opening new doors of ministry for me to walk though. I did not try to open other doors; I waited on God and He opened them. Within two years, God allowed me to be used overseas in revival ministry, and God prompted me to start writing. To be honest, I had never enjoyed writing, but it is amazing how God changes you when He births His ideas in you.

Listening, Abiding, and Obeying

The first step in personal revival, then, is hearing God speak. To hear God speak, we need to be abiding in God's presence with righteousness. When God speaks, we must obey quickly, adjusting our lives to God's voice, His Word. If God speaks a word of correction, we must always remember the point of departure is the point of return. Wherever it was that we stopped striving in our faith, wherever we failed to obey or just tolerated sin, this is the place to which we must return to start afresh with God. There are no shortcuts, no ignoring of the past. We are always required to face up to our mistakes, failures, and pride. We have to learn to live in a holy and humble relationship with God and others.

William C. Burns, a Scottish evangelist and missionary to China in the mid-1800s, said, "Oh, how is it that the Lord's own people have so little perseverance? How is it that when they do enter into their place of prayer to be alone, they are so easily persuaded to be turned away empty; instead of wrestling with God to pour out His Spirit, they retire from the secret place without the answer, and submit it as being God's will."[3] Oh, that we would begin wrestling with God to pour out His Spirit among us.

Additional Scripture on Hearing God

Genesis 3:8–10; Deuteronomy 8:20, 13:17–18; Psalm 29:3–9; Isaiah 6:8–9

Scriptural Prayer for Revival

Initiating Father, just as You spoke to Jacob, I thank You for speaking to me (Genesis 35:1). Let my ears be attentive to Your voice, and let my mind be focused on Your Word. Your Word is truth and nourishment to my soul. Speak to me through Your Word and ignite a revival in my spirit.

Just as Jacob arose in obedience to Your Word, teach me to arise from things that distract me, things that consume my time, energy, and resources so that I may obey You. Show me my sin and cleanse me. Teach me, Father, how to change, how to repent, how to be purified, so I can know You and walk with You (v. 2).

Let repentance flow through me like a mighty river. Give me a hunger for You. Teach me to recall Your faithfulness in times past. As You answered Jacob in the day of his distress, answer me, Lord (v. 3).

Father, teach me to establish reminders of my meeting with You as Jacob did. Let me make spiritual markers, so I won't ever forget our meetings or Your Word (v. 7). Let me build my own personal altar where I can run daily. Thank You for letting me hear Your voice. I praise You. Send revival to me, the church, and our land. All in Jesus' name, amen.

Reflection Questions

1. When was the last time you specifically heard God speaking to you? What did He say? How did you respond? How long did it take you to adjust your life in obedience to what God said?

2. Hebrews 5:11 warns us of becoming a "dull" hearer, lacking sensitivity to the voice of God. What are some things that cause dullness of hearing?

3. We are told in 1 Peter 2:2 to desire the pure milk of the Word. How is your appetite for the Word? How is your hunger and thirst for God visible or obvious in your daily life? What "junk food" do you partake of that does not nourish your soul and spirit?

4. What things distract you from spending time listening to God? How much time do you give to daily Bible reading?

5. What is God speaking to you about in your quiet time? What is He asking you to do differently?

Chapter 2

REVIVAL under MOSES: Experiencing God's Presence

Oh, that You would rend the heavens! That You would come down! That the mountains might shake at Your presence . . .
That the nations may tremble at Your presence!

(Isaiah 64:1–2)

SCRIPTURE:
EXODUS 33:1–4, 7–9, 11, 13–15, 17–18, 20–23

Then the Lord said to Moses, "Depart *and* go up from here, you and the people you have brought out of the land of Egypt, to the land of which I swore to Abraham, Isaac, and Jacob, saying, 'To your descendants I will give it.' And I will send *My* Angel before you, and I will drive out the Canaanite and the Amorite. . . . *Go up* to a land flowing with milk and honey; for I will not go up in your midst, lest I consume you on the way, for you *are* a stiff necked people."

And when the people heard this bad news, they mourned and no one put on his ornaments. . . .

Moses took his tent and pitched it outside the camp, far from the camp, and called it the tabernacle of meeting. And it came to pass *that* everyone who sought the Lord went out to the tabernacle of meeting which *was* outside the camp. So it was, whenever Moses went out to the tabernacle, *that* all the people rose, and each man stood *at* his tent door and watched Moses until he had gone into the tabernacle. And it came to pass, when Moses entered the tabernacle, that the pillar of cloud descended and stood *at* the door of the tabernacle, and *the* LORD talked with Moses. . . . So the LORD spoke to Moses face to face, as a man speaks to his friend . . .

"I pray, if I have found grace in Your sight, show me now Your way, that I may know You and that I may find grace in Your sight. And consider that this nation *is* Your people."

And He said, "My Presence will go *with you*, and I will give you rest."

Then he said to Him, "If Your Presence does not go *with us*, do not bring us up from here.". . .

So the LORD said to Moses, "I will also do this thing that you have spoken; for you have found grace in My sight, and I know you by name."

And he said, "Please, show me Your glory.". . .

But He said, "You cannot see My face . . . and live." And the LORD said, "Here is a place by Me, and you shall stand on the rock. So it shall be, while My glory passes by, that I will put you in the cleft of the rock, and I will cover you with My hand while I pass by. Then I will take away My hand and you shall see My back; but My face shall not be seen."

Experiencing God's Presence

God had led Israel with a pillar of cloud by day and a pillar of fire by night (Exodus 13:21–22). The cloud represented the presence of God with His people. "The glory of the LORD appeared in the cloud" (Exodus 16:10). They came to Mt. Sinai (Exodus 19), and Moses went up and received God's direction and instruction for Israel. Four times in this chapter and once in the next one (Exodus 19:3, 8, 20, 24; 20:21), Moses made the long ascent up into this mountain to receive God's Word and then returned to deliver it.

Then in Exodus 24:9, Moses went up again to receive God's direction and instruction: "Then Moses went up into the mountain, and a cloud covered the mountain. Now the glory of the LORD rested on Mount Sinai, and the cloud covered it six days. And on the seventh day He called to Moses out of the midst of the cloud. . . . So Moses went into the midst of the cloud and went up into the mountain forty days and forty nights" (vv. 15–16, 18).

While Moses was gone for nearly six weeks on the mountain, the children of Israel built a golden calf, an idol, and began to worship it. In doing this, the Israelites committed a terrible sin against God and corrupted themselves. God told Moses what had taken place (Exodus 32:7–8), and Moses returned to Israel's camp and dealt with their sin. According to verse 31, he "returned to the LORD" and interceded for the people as Israel repented of this sin.

Notice that after Israel's sin in chapter 32, we have no mention of the cloud over Israel, which represented God's presence. In the first verse of chapter 33, God commanded Moses and Israel to "depart" and go to the land He promised them, and He would send His Angel before them. Again, no cloud went with them. The cloud "will not go up in your midst" (v. 3).

Seeking Separation

Moses protested, telling God in Gen. 33:15 he did not want to go if

God's presence was not to go with them. Israel had repented of their sin, but sin is costly. Moses felt so strongly that he took the tent of meeting outside the camp and sought the Lord and God's manifest presence as he had experienced it in the cloud. Moses was desperate and burdened. He wanted the presence of God to go with them just as a shepherd would lead, guide, and care for his sheep. Moses longed for the presence of God.

In response, "the pillar of cloud descended and stood at the door of the tabernacle, and the LORD talked with Moses" (v. 9). Oh, that we would have such a desire for God's presence in our lives and our churches. Oh, that we would be so burdened, so desperate, that we would seek a place separate from others so we can pray without distraction for God's presence to be among us.

As Moses experienced the presence of God, the people saw the pillar of cloud, and it prompted each of them to worship (v. 10). Revival is all about the presence of God. It is the demonstration of God's presence. It is His glory in the church. Without the presence of God, the church is nothing more than a social club or a benevolent society. We must long and hunger for God's manifested presence, both personally and corporately. Israel, as they observed Moses, understood the necessity of God's presence. Do we?

The word "presence" in this passage is the Hebrew word *paniym,* which means "face." The presence of God is the idea of us being pleasing in His sight. The Greek word for "pleasing" means "to put a smile on the face of the one you love."

Do you live in such a way as to put a smile on God's face? Do you live in such a way, in deed and word, as to put a smile on the face of Christ?

In October 1997, *USA Today* reported on a survey conducted by

Roper Starch Worldwide, asking Americans in the top one percent income bracket how much they would be willing to spend on several intangible items, including great intellect, true love, and a place in heaven. Researchers found that the super wealthy would be willing to spend an average of $407,000 for great intellect; $487,000 for true love; and $640,000 for a place in heaven.[4] The Bible tells us that wealth can buy many things, but it cannot buy you a place in heaven nor can it secure God's presence for you on earth.

Distancing Ourselves from Distraction

It is so easy to get distracted from God and caught up in things of little value. When we get distracted, the presence of God seems so far away. Do you realize distractions create distance between us and God? When you are experiencing a season of dryness, listen to God's instruction to Moses. God told Moses to drive out the enemies. What enemies are distracting you from the purpose and plan of God?

The devil comes at all of us. He comes as a roaring lion (1 Peter 5:8) to scare, intimidate, and devour. His goal is to kill, steal, and destroy (John 10:10). He is crafty enough to know when he cannot touch us. Then, he tries to get us to compromise, so he comes as an angel of light (2 Corinthians 11:14). This angel of light lures us away, seduces us with good things, fun things, until we have left the place God has for us. Once away from God, we are susceptible to the devil's attacks. It is your responsibility and mine not to be lured away into the devil's trap. Be careful and cautious.

Our churches suffer when we are not living in God's presence. Ted S. Rendell said, "Perhaps the greatest barrier to revival on a large scale is the fact that we are too interested in a great display. We want the exhibition; God is looking for a man who will throw himself entirely upon God. Whenever self-effort, self-glory, self-seeking, or self-promotion enters into the work of revival, then God leaves us to ourselves."[5]

We can begin our day with a lot of religious activity, but if we fail to secure the presence of God with confidence, our lives will not be impacted and we will not know God's leading. We desperately need the presence of God in our midst. It is each Christian's responsibility to secure God's presence. Revival is all about the presence of God among His people.

How do we secure the presence of God? Do not be in a hurry. Slow down your quiet time. Wait upon the Lord. Give Him time and opportunity to speak to your spirit while you are still and quiet before Him. You do not have to be talking all the time. Wait in silent expectation, read the Word of God slowly, write it out if you need to. Sing hymns or praise songs to the Lord. But above all, listen. Relate what you are going through to your prayers and the verses you are reading.

Getting Personal

As I think about how strong the presence of God was during the Florida revival I described earlier, I am overwhelmed with the knowledge that I am not capable of capturing it in words. In all honesty, God's presence was the revival. (You can read more about that particular revival in my book *The Forty Day Reign of God*.) As the revival in Florida was extended, God continued pouring out His presence upon us heavily. It was so strong that the church asked my wife and me for permission to fly our children there, so they could experience it also.

Our children were fourteen and eleven years old at the time, and neither had been born again. They had been in church all their lives, attended Christian school, but still were not saved. We agreed with some hesitancy for them to fly for the first time alone and without an adult. They arrived safe and sound on Friday morning. The services started at 7:00 p.m. each evening, but at 6:30 my wife and I were called to the host pastor's office. There sat both of our kids, tears dripping off their chins. The conviction of God was evidenced. They were calling out to God to save their souls. It was truly an amazing moment. Even as wonderful and amazing as that moment was, it pales in comparison to the presence of God that was moving in that revival. The presence of God is everything. Even the salvation of my children cannot compare to God's manifest presence in our midst.

A year or so after the Florida revival, God poured out His presence in a Tennessee church in a mighty revival. The people and I met every day for forty days, and the revival atmosphere lasted eleven months. In this revival, the presence of God was tremendous, too. After the first few nights and many hours of conviction and confession, we felt that the roof of the church was being split open to allow God's presence to rain down. It was an unexpected and astoundingly real feeling. There was one area on the altar with a circumference of about ten feet where God's presence was especially strong and magnified. When we stood in this area, many others and I felt as if our bodies were elevated to another level, like we were standing at the opening of a stairway to heaven. People were naturally drawn to this area, and the most desperate and broken were restored here. This area and the entire altar became holy ground: a place of extreme reverence, sanctification, refuge, and release.

It was also a place of comfort, hope, and union with God. God's presence was manifested as an expression of evident joy. People looked more joyful than they might look at important life events, such as a marriage or baby's birth. Why? This joy was cultivated by an un-quenchable longing for worship, praise, and preaching. We could not pray long enough. We would lie before God, soaking in the beautiful, wonderful, and amazing presence of God. Psalm 16:11 says, "In Your presence is fullness of joy." When you know the presence of God, you know revival.

Additional Scripture on Experiencing God's Presence

Genesis 4:16; Exodus 33:4–15; Psalm 16:11, 95:2; Jude 1:24–25

Scriptural Prayer for Revival

Loving Father, revival is about Your presence being real in my life and in the church. Oh, Lord, let me know Your presence. Manifest Your presence in my life and in my church. Lord, send revival. Teach me to be sensitive to Your voice. When You tell me to depart, to get away from the ungodly influences of my world, enable me to obey quickly as Moses did (Exodus 33:1).

Father, drive out the enemies of Your people, expose them for what and who they are. In my community, expose those who oppose and resist You. In the political arena, local governments, schools, and churches, expose those who oppose You and drive them out (v. 2).

Show me how I am stiff-necked and stubborn. Enable me to yield those areas to You (v. 3).

Show me that special place of meeting with You where I can run, that place where I can get away from the distractions of life and be alone to meet You. Oh, Lord, let others see my devotion to You, not to brag or puff myself up, but for Your glory (vv. 7–8).

Father, put a separation between me and the outside world, as You did with Moses. Put Your pillar between me and the distractions of life, so I can commune uninterrupted with You (v. 9).

Speak to me as You did to Moses. Let Your Word, Your truth, be ever consuming my mind. Father, I long to be Your friend (v. 11). I long to know You. Let me find grace in Your sight (v. 13). I long for Your presence. Teach me to seek Your presence, and show me any substitutes I have made for You (v. 15).

Father, just as You knew Moses' name, thank You for knowing my name. Thank You for hearing and answering my prayers (v. 17).

Give me spiritual eyes, Father, to behold Your glory, just as You did Moses. Show me anything that hinders my walk with You and separate me unto You (v. 18).

Teach me separation. Show me my place by You. Enable me to be still and wait on You. Let me know Your presence. Cover me with Your hand (v. 21). Place me on the rock that does not move. You are my Rock. In life, I may shake and quiver, but my Rock never does. Father, You are honey in the rock. Thank You (v. 22).

Father, forgive me of my sin. Burden me to intercede for the church and give me joy in prayer and a desire to pray. Move in me and through me for Your glory. Let others see Your work in my life and in the church. Send revival to Your people. In Jesus' name, amen.

Reflection Questions

1. Have you ever experienced the manifest presence of God? In your church? If so, how would you describe that experience?

2. Is being aware of God's presence important enough to you that you refuse to go through a day without it? What do you need to do today to secure God's presence?

3. Is there something or someone else's presence acting as a sub-

stitute for God's presence in your life? What or who is it? Why do you allow it?

4. Are you content as you are? Is merely being "religious" enough for you? In Romans 8:29, we are told that God's will for us is to be conformed to the image of Jesus Christ. When you are in God's presence, He is best able to make you like Jesus. Is that happening in your life? Why or why not?

5. What is God saying to you today?

Chapter 3

REVIVAL under the JUDGES:
Reaching Desperation

So it was, when the captains of the chariots saw
Jehoshaphat, that they said, "It is the king of Israel!"
Therefore they surrounded him to attack; but Jehoshaphat
cried out, and the LORD helped him, and God diverted
them from him. (2 CHRONICLES 18:31)

SCRIPTURE:
JUDGES 3:1, 3–4, 6–9

Now these *are* the nations which the LORD left, that He might
test Israel by them, *that is*, all who had not known any of the
wars in Canaan. . . . [F]ive lords of the Philistines . . . were *left,*
that He might test Israel by them, to know whether they would
obey the commandments of the LORD, which He had commanded their fathers by the hand of Moses. . . . And they took
their daughters to be their wives, and gave their daughters to
their sons; and they served their gods. So the children of Israel
did evil in the sight of the LORD. They forgot the LORD their God,
and served the Baals and Asherahs. Therefore the anger of the
LORD was hot against Israel, and He sold them into the hand of
Cushan-Rishathaim king of Mesopotamia; and the children of

Israel served Cushan-Rishathaim eight years. When the children of Israel cried out to the LORD, the LORD raised up a deliverer for the children of Israel, who delivered them.

Reaching Desperation

When a friend of mine was a teenager, he fell out of a boat into water that was over his head, but he could not swim. He thrashed and struggled. Despite all his efforts, he went under. At that moment, nothing was important to him except oxygen. He desperately needed air. Money didn't matter, neither did fame or his appearance or his relationships with others. When he managed to break the surface, he gasped, filling his lungs with air.

Have you ever been that desperate for God? Many people cry out but not necessarily to God. They cry out to family and friends, counterfeit or false gods, to the government, and even to angels. Their motivation is self.

The children of Israel cried out in Exodus 2, but the Bible does not say they cried out to God. Exodus 14 is the first mention that they cried out to God. To cry out to God is an act of desperation. Crying out to God is also an act of faith in the God who can and will deliver. Crying out to God in desperation positions us to embrace God in revival.

Six times the phrase "the children of Israel cried unto the LORD" occurs in the book of Judges. These six occurrences represent five seasons of defeat and bondage. The Israelites all too quickly forgot Moses' warnings in Deuteronomy 8 and 30, which tell us if they forget the Lord, He will turn them over to the enemy, and they will be tormented. They forgot the warning of Leviticus 26:27–28: "If you don't obey Me, but walk contrary to Me, then I will also walk contrary to you in fury, and I, even I, will chastise you seven times for your sins." There is a cost to forsaking and disobeying God.

Israel did evil in the sight of the Lord. What does that mean? Basically, they held an attitude contrary to God's will and became involved in activities against His Word. They took up the world's gods, and in doing so, refused the one true God.

For Israel, things would go well for a while and they would enjoy the blessing of God. Soon, however, they would grow comfortable, and then they would begin to mimic their pagan neighbors. As they forsook God, He allowed them to experience difficulties and become captive to those nations and people that did not know or serve God. After years of this bondage and oppression, the children of Israel repented, crying out to God. He heard them and sent them a deliverer.

The judges came on the scene to proclaim God's message of restoration. We see this cycle repeated about every forty years over an estimated two-hundred-year period. The desperate cry of God's children moved God. That same cry today when we stray and return in repentance still moves God. Desperation moves us to cry out to the only One who can save and deliver us—God.

Getting Personal

Desperation should cause us to get honest with God. During the Florida revival I described in the previous chapter, many people appeared desperate for God, even the host pastor. He was so desperate that he asked the entire congregation to prayerfully examine themselves and confess any sin. Things got quiet and still as sins were expressed openly. Finally, one man said, "We mistreated a former staff member, our former youth pastor. We owe him and his family an apology. We need to seek his forgiveness. We need to make things right." Others agreed, yet no one knew where he was or how to reach him, but they drafted a letter of apology so it would be ready when they located him.

A few weeks after that meeting, a member of that church was attending an "Experiencing God" weekend and the leader asked those attending to share what God was doing in their churches. This man could not wait to share how mightily God was moving. As he shared about people being saved and lives transformed, he also told how they had hurt and offended a former staff member. He said they were trying to locate the man to apologize. Suddenly, from the back of the room, a man started to weep audibly and uncontrollably.

The room became quiet. The weeping man said, "That's me. I'm that former youth pastor." There was stunned silence for a moment and then reconciliation poured forth.

One pastor's sense of desperation for his church to be right with God led to reconciliation and forgiveness. A burden was lifted as one church sought to get right with a former staff member, so that they could continue moving forward with God.

When we get comfortable in our service to God, that's when we need to be cautious. You cannot be comfortable and desperate at the same time. Spiritual desperation comes only when we realize nothing, absolutely nothing, can satisfy us other than Jesus Christ. When we cry out to God in desperation, God will respond. But then we must follow. Where and how He will lead is amazing. G. Campbell Morgan said, "We cannot organize revival, but we can set our sails to catch the wind from heaven when God chooses to blow upon His people again."[6]

Additional Scripture on Desperation

Exodus 14:10; Psalm 27:3–5; Jeremiah 17:7; Matthew 20:30

Scriptural Prayer for Revival

Powerful Father, just as in the time of the judges, we need revival—revival in our lives, in our churches, in our land. Oh, God, I cry out to You to send revival.

Father, we live in a pampered society. People do not know what it is to struggle in and for their faith. Just as in the time of the judges, we must learn to fight for our faith. Just as You left people in the land to test Israel, give me wisdom to understand what things You have placed in my life to test and build my faith. Enable me to pass those tests (Judges 3:1).

Father, show me things and people that I allow to turn my heart from You, and let me separate myself from them. Give me the courage to end relationships and separate myself from those who pull me away from You. Show me the relationships that drain my faith instead of building it (v. 3).

Please give me wisdom not to sacrifice my children to people who have no heart for You.

Father, teach me desperation for You. Have I grown comfortable in my sin? Have I grown accustomed to the bondage of the world? Have I forsaken obedience to You? May I live in complete obedience to Your Word. That means I must spend massive amounts of time in Your Word. Give me a fresh hunger for Your Word (v. 4).

Show me what I am giving my children to. Is it the gods of this world? Is it fashion, pleasure, sports, entertainment? Forgive me for over emphasizing these things and not having a true, obedient heart for You. Oh God, break my addiction to these things (v. 6).

Father, have I forgotten You and done evil in Your sight by not giving You my time and attention? Show me my evil ways, thoughts and attitudes (v. 7).

Just as Your anger was stirred against Israel, Father, show me what in my life stirs Your anger against me. Show me if I am in bondage to this world or the world's system. Show me the ways I have adopted the world's mindset and values. Please do not give me over to the world. Deal with me. Send warnings in my life if I begin to love the world (v. 8). When I have to go from one thing, event, or activity to another to find satisfaction, let me realize I am in bondage. When pleasing people and getting their approval is extremely important to me, let me realize I am in bondage.

Father, I cry out to You, deliver me. Forgive me of my sin and cleanse me. I cry out to You, oh God. I am desperate for You to work in my life and in my church (v. 9). Lord, I need revival. Teach me perseverance, Lord. Teach me not to quit. Move in my behalf. Lord, send revival to Your people. In Jesus' name, amen.

Reflection Questions

1. To be desperate means you are almost giving up hope. Have you ever been in that position financially? Emotionally? Spiritually? What did you do?

2. Does your lifestyle testify of the absolute authority of Scripture? In what ways?

3. How has the world tried to overcome you? Do you wait until you are completely overcome by the world to cry out to God?

4. What things break your heart for God?

5. When times of distress come, do you generally cry out to God, or do you try to figure it out on your own? Why?

6. What is God saying to you today?

Chapter 4

REVIVAL under SAMUEL: Confessing

And I prayed to the Lord my God, and made confession,
and said, "O Lord, great and awesome God who keeps His
covenant and mercy with those who love Him, and with
those who keep His commandments." (Daniel 9:4)

SCRIPTURE:
1 SAMUEL 7:1–13

Then the men of Kirjath Jearim came and took the ark of the
Lord, and brought it into the house of Abinadab on the hill, and
consecrated Eleazar his son to keep the ark of the Lord. So it
was that the ark remained in Kirjath Jearim a long time; it was
there twenty years. And all the house of Israel lamented after
the Lord.

Then Samuel spoke to all the house of Israel saying, "If you
return to the Lord with all your hearts, *then* put away the foreign
gods and the Ashtoreths from among you, and prepare your
hearts for the Lord, and serve Him only; and He will deliver you
from the hand of the Philistines." So the children of Israel put
away the Baals and the Ashtoreths, and served the Lord only.

And Samuel said, "Gather all Israel to Mizpah, and I will pray
to the Lord for you." So they gathered together at Mizpah, drew
water, and poured *it* out before the Lord. And they fasted that

day, and said there, "We have sinned against the Lord." And Samuel judged the children of Israel at Mizpah.

Now when the Philistines heard the children of Israel had gathered together at Mizpah, the lords of the Philistines went up against Israel. And when the children of Israel heard of it, they were afraid of the Philistines. . . . So the children of Israel said to Samuel, "Do not cease to cry out to the Lord our God for us, that He may save us from the hand of the Philistines."

And Samuel took a suckling lamb and offered *it as* a whole burnt offering to the Lord. Then Samuel cried out to the Lord for Israel, and the Lord answered him. Now as Samuel was offering up the burnt offering, the Philistines drew near to battle against Israel. But the Lord thundered with a loud thunder upon the Philistines that day, and so confused them that they were overcome before Israel. And the men of Israel went out of Mizpah and pursued the Philistines, and drove them back as far as below Beth Car. Then Samuel took a stone and set *it* up between Mizpah and Shen, and called its name Ebenezer, saying, "Thus far the Lord has helped us."

So the Philistines were subdued, and they did not come anymore into the territory of Israel. And the hand of the Lord was against the Philistines all the days of Samuel.

Confessing Honestly

Psalm 32:3 tells us how David felt when he failed to confess: "When I kept silent, my bones grew old, Through my groaning all the day long." There is nothing that takes the joy out of life like unconfessed sin. Confession is a key principle of experiencing God in revival. It is a fruit of repentance. In Revelation 2, the church of Ephesus was to repent and to do her first works. According to Acts 19:18, her first works were confession of sin and revealing deeds. Many also burned their books on sorcery. As a result, the Word of God grew mightily and prevailed. Confession is an experience God allows us to go through so we can walk in communion with Him. In revival, confession of sin becomes the norm.

In Scripture, we are told to confess with our mouths the Lord Jesus Christ (Romans 10:9), to confess our sin (1 John 1:9), and to confess our trespasses to one another (James 5:16). In the Greek, "to confess to God" means "to agree with God,"[7] or "to say the same thing." It means not merely confessing intellectually, but rather a confession wrought by the convicting of the Holy Spirit, knowing we have wronged our God. Confession of sin is not easy. Our flesh fights against it. Our pride wants to hold onto our dignity or even our sin. To walk with God, however, we must learn to daily confess sin.

E. M. Bounds said: "Revivals are among the charter rights of the Church. . . . A revival means a heart-broken pastor. A revival means a church on its knees confessing its sins—the sins of the individual and of the Church—confessing the sins of the times and of the community."[8]

We are not only to confess our sins to God but also to others. When my activity or attitude affects other people, I am responsible to confess to them. The sphere of confession is limited to the sphere of the influence.

Samuel was raised in a time when the Word of God was rare (1 Samuel 3:1). He had to learn to hear God speak and recognize His voice. We must do the same. We can learn to distinguish God's voice by its content. The content will acknowledge the holiness of God, and the guidance of God always agrees with Scripture.

Later, in chapter 7, Samuel instructed the people of God about how to return to God, serve Him, and prepare their hearts. One of the keys in returning to God and experiencing revival is honest confession. David tells us in Psalm 81:15, "The haters of the LORD would *pretend submission* to Him" (emphasis mine). Let us not be guilty of pretending submission.

Receiving Cleansing

First John 1:9 says to confess and receive forgiveness. Forgiveness and cleansing is not the same thing. Forgiveness comes immediately as honest, wholehearted confession of sin is made to God. Cleansing comes only as you reclaim ground you surrendered to Satan when you sinned. To reclaim the ground and experience the cleansing of God, you have to surrender that area back to God afresh and anew. "If we walk in the light as He is in the light, we have fellowship with one another, and the blood of Jesus Christ His Son cleanses us from all sin" (1 John 1:7). The point is God does not forgive sin in a void. We must change our direction. We must leave the darkness and come to the light. That is repentance. Cleansing requires the repentance of sin. If you are not in fellowship with your Christian brother or sister, you have not repented and have not been cleansed. Repent, come to the light of Christ and confess your sin. Allow the blood of Jesus to cover and cleanse every stain. Then we can know true revival.

Getting Personal

In my Florida revival experience, as God continued to move, one night a man stood beside the pastor of the church, weeping. He confessed his sin to God, the pastor, and the entire church. He stated he had been the ring leader in trying to have the pastor removed. He had been involved in secret meetings, intending only to harm the pastor. He asked the pastor to forgive him.

The pastor embraced and forgave him. Then the man asked the church to forgive him, and the church also extended forgiveness. Next, the pastor, that man, and others gathered on their knees, seeking cleansing and restoration. They rose up, still weeping but praising God for the victory He gave that night.

In the Tennessee revival I described in my book *The Forty Day Reign of God*, confession began in solemn assemblies prior to the revival. Deep within people's hearts a yearning began to grow, igniting a desire to be completely clean and pure before God. Once revival began and God rained down His presence, the embers burst into fires of conviction that destroyed all pride, embarrassment, and shame. God's sweet breath fueled the confessions and provided the life necessary to sustain heartache and humiliation.

People wept at the altar, broken from their sin. They fell on their faces in repentance. They confessed sins that had taken place twenty or fifty years in the past. We never asked anyone to give public confession of sin. God drew them to the altar to plead publically. With each confession, we could sense the release of a heavy burden and feel the freedom that comes with knowing God's forgiveness. The joy of salvation became visible.

Additional Scripture on Confessing

Joshua 7:19; 2 Chronicles 30:22; Ezra 10:11; Romans 10:9

Scriptural Prayer for Revival

Faithful Father, just as in Samuel's day, it seems as if Your word is rare. There is so much media-weakened gospel, but Lord, I long for a fresh word from You.

Father, to lament means to feel or express sorrow or regret. Just as Israel lamented after You, teach me to mourn aloud, to lament after You (1 Samuel 7:2).

And teach me what it means to return to You with all my heart. Teach me what I must put away, what I must put off and put on. Father, show me how to prepare my heart for You (v. 3).

Oh Father, send revival. Stir honest confession in my soul. Teach me to deny myself, so I can spend time seeking You in prayer. Teach me to fast, not only from food but from time robbers, such as television and the Internet. Intensify my desperation for You. Oh God, I miss You. I am the one who has moved away. Restore me, Lord. Show me my sin. I confess my sin; I confess my indifference to You. Show me how to return to You with all my heart. Show me the things of the world that I have embraced that are sin (v. 6).

Lord, let me not be afraid of the world as Israel was, but let me be wise, discerning, and cautious of the world (v. 7).

Let me know the great need I have to be open and honest with others, to ask others to pray for me. It is pride when I fail to do this. Forgive me (v. 8).

Father, as Samuel offered a sacrifice and cried out to You, let me truly understand Jesus Christ was the Lamb sacrificed, and by His blood I have access to You (v. 9). Teach me what it is to sacrifice unto You. Lord, move mightily on behalf of Your people. Answer me as I sacrifice to You (v. 10).

Father, I pray You will consume those who oppose You, just as You did the Philistines in Samuel's day. Teach me to acknowledge Your mighty acts. Let me set up stones of remembrance, markers of Your help, deliverance, and Your great faithfulness (v. 12).

May I recognize Your voice, Your promptings, and help me obey quickly. Show me anyone I need to go to and seek forgiveness or to make restitution. Father, hear my confession and restore me. In Jesus' name, amen.

Reflection Questions

1. No amount of tears, prayers, or protests is a substitute for honest confession. In confession, we get honest with ourselves and God. Why is such honesty difficult?

2. Is there any known sin in your life? Pet sins, willful sins, hidden sins? Things you tolerate but know are wrong. Why? What are they?

3. Do you engage in selective obedience? What does God want you to do about these situations?

4. When was the last time you confessed your sin to others?

5. When was the last time you asked anyone to pray for you, being specific about an area of need?

6. Be quiet before the Lord. What is He saying to you today?

Chapter 5

REVIVAL under the SONS of KORAH: Bearing Testimony

By faith Enoch was taken away so that he did not see death,
"and was not found, because God had taken him";
for before he was taken he had this testimony,
that he pleased God. (HEBREWS 11:5)

SCRIPTURE:
PSALM 85:1–7

LORD, You have been favorable to Your land; You have brought back the captivity of Jacob. You have forgiven the iniquity of Your people; You have covered all their sin. Selah. You have taken away all Your wrath; You have turned from the fierceness of Your anger.

Restore us, O God of our salvation. And cause Your anger toward us to cease. Will You be angry with us forever? Will You prolong Your anger to all generations? Will You not revive us again, That Your people may rejoice in You? Show us Your mercy, LORD, And grant us Your salvation.

Bearing Testimony

Polycarp was a disciple of the apostle John and an early church leader whose life ended when he refused to betray his Lord. Asked one last time to disavow Christ, the old man replied, "Eighty and six years have I served Him, and He has done me no wrong. How can I speak evil of my King who saved me?"[9] Even in his death, he testified of Christ.

Every born again person has a testimony. In fact, we have many testimonies. We have a salvation testimony. We have a testimony of God's provision, healing, or deliverance. Our testimony always is to honor and exalt God the Father of our Lord Jesus Christ.

It is this testimony we are to be proclaiming to the world. We are to testify (to tell forth) what we know and have experienced in Christ Jesus. This testimony is always Christ centered and Christ honoring. It is not human centered or human exalting.

In revival, bearing testimony to the glory of God is contagious. It flows as we know His presence and movement in our lives. Testifying is not done by the prompting of humans, but by the prompting of the Holy Spirit. It is done for God's glory.

The sons of Korah were the descendants of the man who rebelled against Moses and Aaron in Numbers 16. The ground opened and swallowed them when they contended against the Lord. Thank God, Korah's descendants did not follow his example. They became the gatekeepers and the singers of the tabernacle. A gatekeeper is one who gives access. Oh, that we would be giving access to others for Christ by testifying of His greatness and showing others the way to revival. Having learned the lesson of the holiness of God, Korah's descendants were faithful to the Lord. We do not have to follow in the footsteps of our forefathers if they refused to obey God. We can start a brand new path.

In Psalm 85, the children of Israel had returned from Babylonian captivity, so the passage is a prayer for the afflicted people of God to know the mercy and favor of God once again. They begin by giving testimony of the greatness of God. "Lord, You have been favorable to Your land. You have brought back the captivity of Jacob. You have forgiven the iniquity of Your people. You have covered all their sin." After they bear testimony to the greatness of God, they begin to pray. Their prayer was for a national revival. Oh, that we also would pray for a national revival in our land.

Getting Personal

As the revival continued in Tennessee, testimonies became spontaneous. People shared their encounters with God. Two churches, one in Kentucky and one in a neighboring Tennessee county, asked our people to come and share with them. Both churches were about one hour's drive away. So on two different occasions, we sent a team of three or four laypeople to give testimony of what God was doing in our church and in their lives.

They testified of the goodness and mercy of almighty God. They shared how they watched as God moved in our midst and how people responded by confessing their sin. They spoke of broken lives being restored. They shared personally of how they were freed from old hurts, bondage, and addictions. As these people shared, hearts began to open. Excitement and expectance moved into those churches. A hunger for more of God began to develop. Why? Because testimonies of the mighty moving of God were shared. And if God could do this in our obscure church, then God could do this anywhere. The power of someone bearing testimony is tremendous. It pulsates with life.

Additional Scripture on Bearing Testimony

2 Chronicles 20:15; Matthew 5:14–16; 1 Corinthians 1:4–7; Revelation 1:9, 12:11

Scriptural Prayer for Revival

Sovereign God, move in my life so that I cannot remain silent. Do not let the rocks and trees cry out to You because I am silent. Let me testify of Your greatness and glory. I praise You for all Your blessings, Father. I praise You for Your favor You show toward me. I praise You for Your mercy. Thank You. Your favor is Your good pleasure on my life (Psalm 85:1).

I exalt you as my God and King. Continue to show me areas of my life that are not pleasing to You. Make me sensitive to my sin, and let me be broken over it. Forgive me, God, for my iniquity, and forgive the iniquity of Your people (v. 2).

Just as the psalmist gave testimony of You, let me testify to others of what You have done in my life. Forgive me for my past silence. Let me understand how the blood of Christ has covered my sin, and let me understand it is based on His blood that I can come to You in prayer (v. 2).

Teach me repentance. Don't turn Your wrath toward me (v. 3). Restore me to You, oh, God. Let me know Your good pleasure and not Your anger (v. 4).

Revive me again. Revive Your church again (v. 6). Let rejoicing fill my mouth and my life. Show me Your mercy, and grant that I may know Your mercy fresh every day (v. 7). Let me see the world through Your eyes. Sanctify me in truth. Let me walk in Your pathway, so my life is a testimony unto You. Father, revive us again, and let a new season of revival spring forth from You. In Jesus' name, amen.

Reflection Questions

1. When was the last time you shared your personal testimony, and with whom did you share it? Have you told your children your testimony of faith in Christ? If not, why not?

2. What circumstances create opportunities to share our testimonies?

3. Who has God placed in your life that needs to hear your testimony? What similar struggles have you experienced?

4. We speak of things important to us. Why is it so difficult to speak about Jesus Christ?

5. If our activities do not match our words, our testimony is silent. Is there an area in your life that would silence you from sharing your testimony? If so, what is it?

6. What is God saying to you today?

Chapter 6

REVIVAL under ASA: Fearing God

The fear of the Lord is the beginning of knowledge, But fools despise wisdom and instruction. (PROVERBS 1:7)

SCRIPTURE:
2 CHRONICLES 14:1–4, 7–9, 11–12, 14; 15:1–2, 8, 10, 12–15

So Abijah rested with his fathers and they buried him in the City of David. Then Asa his son reigned in his place. In his days the land was quiet for ten years. Asa did *what was* good and right in the eyes of the LORD his God, for he removed the altars of the foreign *gods* and the high places, and broke down the *sacred* pillars and cut down the wooden images. He commanded Judah to seek the LORD God of their fathers, and to observe the law and the commandments. . . . Therefore he said to Judah, ". . . because we have sought the LORD our God; we have sought *Him*, and He has given us rest on every side.". . . And Asa had an army of three hundred thousand. . . .

Then Zerah the Ethiopian came out against them with an army of a millionmen. . . . And Asa cried out to the LORD his God, and said "LORD, *it is* nothing for You to help, whether with many or with those who have no power; help us, O LORD our God, for we rest on You, and in Your name we go against this multitude.

O Lord, You *are* our God; do not let man prevail against You!"

So the Lord struck the Ethiopians before Asa and Judah. . . . Then they defeated all the cities around Gerar, for the fear of the Lord came upon them. . . .

Now the Spirit of God came upon Azariah the son of Obed. And he went out to meet Asa, and said to him: "Hear me, Asa, and all Judah and Benjamin. The Lord *is* with you while you are with Him. If you seek Him, He will be found by you; but if you forsake Him, He will forsake you . . .

And when Asa heard these words and the prophecy of Obed the prophet, he took courage . . . and he restored the altar of the Lord. . . .

So they gathered together at Jerusalem in the third month. . . . Then they entered into a covenant to seek the Lord God of their fathers with all their heart and with all their soul; and whoever would not seek the Lord God of Israel was put to death, whether small or great, whether man or woman. Then they took an oath before the Lord with a loud voice, with shouting and trumpets and rams' horns. And all Judah rejoiced at the oath, for they had sworn with their heart and sought Him with all their soul; and He was found by them, and the Lord gave them rest all around.

Fearing God

When Adam and Eve sinned in the Garden of Eden and became separated from God, one of the consequences was fear. Fear is a psychological problem that resulted from man's sin. Humans have developed many fears since the fall in Genesis 3. Some fears may be understandable, but many are not. Agoraphobia is the fear of crowded places. Doraphobia is the fear of animal skins or furs. Trypanophobia is the fear of injections. Triskaidekaphobia is the fear of the number thirteen.

The one fear that delivers humans from all other fears is the fear of God. When this fear is rightly understood and lived by, we need not fear anything else. Every day we must choose between the fear of humans and the fear of God. The fear of God comes to us at the moment of salvation. Just as we receive the Spirit of God, God places in us His fear (Jeremiah 32:39). When we fear God, it shows in how we live. To fear God means to cherish an awesome sense of His greatness, His grandeur, and His excellence. We act on what we have in our hearts.

One of the greatest gifts we can leave our children, and the next generation, is a godly testimony of faith in Christ, as evidenced by how we fear God. If we have had a foundation of faith laid for us, praise God. If we have not had this, we still must press on in Christ Jesus. We are accountable to seek God and honor Him with all our being.

Asa was a king who had a mixed heritage. His great-granddad was King David, the man after God's own heart. His granddad was King Solomon, a man compromised with lust. His father was King Abijah, who was idolatrous. Even though they all served God with their mouths, it was their actions that proved their faith or their faithlessness and whether they truly feared the Lord.

Two Kinds of Fear of God

In the midst a crisis, against innumerable odds, Asa and all of Judah sought after and cried out to God, and they were victorious. The "fear of the LORD came upon them; and they plundered all" (14:14). The fear of the Lord is one of the enablements of God for us to face the enemy and overcome. In a lost person, the fear of the Lord is consum-ing dread of God. When Asa and his armies attacked the cities around Gerar, the fear of the Lord, a dread, came on all those pagan villages. They were literally afraid of Jehovah God, and with good reason.

But for Asa and Judah, the people of God, the fear of the Lord was not a dread, but a reverential awe of God. They cherished that sense of the greatness and grandeur of God. When we have the fear of God in our lives, we reverence, respect, and honor God. We will seek God.

Such fear of God means we know the character of God. He is God, sovereign, holy, great, and awesome. We understand our ob-ligation to God: to love Him, obey Him, and trust Him. Finally, as we fear God, we gain a pervasive sense of the presence of God. This sense of God's presence has a controlling effect on a person because we know He is with us.

Asa served God when God's people were under attack by the world (14:9). It is no different today. What are we to do? We are to do the same thing that Asa did. We cry out to God, asking Him for help. He is Jehovah Ezer (Psalm 33:20), the Lord our Helper. Then we are to recount the greatness, faithfulness, and power of God in our past. He saved you and sustains you. He has provided for you and He has protected you, even when you were unaware of it.

God often tests His children for the purpose of building their faith in Him. The test is never meant to make us rely on our flesh, friends, or family. We are tested so that our faith in God increases. We are tested to show if we will seek the Lord or forsake Him. We are tested so the fear of God can be displayed in our lives. When the other nations heard of the power of God and the victory He gave Asa, they feared God also (14:14). This fear was a terror because our God is an awesome God.

Getting Personal

What would make a person openly confess a humiliating and terrible sin to his church? Only one thing: a consuming desire to be right with God. In one of the revivals I experienced, a middle-aged man came up and said, "I have to confess my sin." He was weeping and could hardly speak. We had asked no one for a public confession. I told him he did not have to share anything publically. But he insisted, "If I am ever to be right with God, I have to share."

I asked him what he needed to confess. He hung his head in shame and said, "I have babies in heaven. I paid to have them aborted." He wept bitterly. I asked him if his wife knew this, to which he replied, "No." I advised him that he needed to tell his wife before he told anyone. He agreed. I called her over to us, and he confessed his sin to her.

This godly woman fell to her knees and began praying for the mothers of those babies.

Then in brokenness, shame, and humiliation, the man made the painful confession to his church and asked us to forgive him.

If I am ever going to be right with God, I have to share, to obey. Why do that?

Because I fear God and since I fear God, I have to do whatever He asks. When God asks us to deal with sin and do things that are not comfortable, we must obey. If we do not obey, then we do not fear God, nor will we continue with God.

Another man responded to an invitation many years ago in my church. As he came to me, he fell on my neck, weeping and wailing. I counseled him, and eventually he stood and shared what God had done for him that day.

A few weeks later another man at that service related what else had happened that day. He had been sitting by a teenage boy. When the man went forward, wailing and weeping, he heard this teenage boy say under his breath, "I will never do that."

"If I am ever to be right with God, I must confess my sin." That's God's way. It honors God. God initiates this. The world thinks, *I will never do that. I will never humiliate myself in such a fashion. I will set my own terms on meeting God.* That is part of our problem today. The devil has led us to believe that we get to decide how we come to God. You cannot set your terms or conditions on coming to God or walking with God. Whatever God calls us to do, He enables us to do, and we must do it. The fear of God enables us to walk in obedience to Christ. A mark of true personal revival is daily living in, and with, the fear of God.

Additional Scripture on Fearing God

Psalm 19:9, 22:23, 25:14, 34:11, 111:10; Proverbs 1:29, 2:5, 10:27, 14:27; Jeremiah 32:38–41

Scriptural Prayer for Revival

Lord Most High, for revival to come, I need to seek You. I praise You for the seasons of rest You give. Let me not waste them or use them for selfish reasons, but allow me the sense to use them for times of kingdom building and preparation for further service, just as Asa did (2 Chronicles 14:1).

Lord, change my heart; give me a surrendered heart, a hungry heart to know You. Show me excuses I make for not serving You and not being faithful to Your church. Show me the idols I have allowed and hidden in my heart. By faith, let me remove them (v. 3). Father, teach me to seek You and obey Your Word (v. 4).

Lord, I praise You for Your faithfulness, Your mercy, and Your protection and provision (v. 7).

Let me not be overwhelmed by the great numbers that oppose me. You are my God (vv. 8–9). Just as You did with Asa, let opposition drive me to seek You. Father, You are my refuge (v. 9). Teach me to trust and rest in You as I cry out to You and obey You (v. 11).

Father, will You manifest Your fear in my life? It has been there since salvation, but allow it to be seen and recognized by those around me. Grow Your fear in me to completion (v. 14).

Lord, I praise You for Your Word and ask You to continue speaking to me. When Your Word comes to me through a human agent, let me receive it (15:1). I praise You. Let Your Spirit move on me. Teach me to abide in You always (v. 2).

Show me anything You have told me in the past that I have failed to do. Lord, narrow the focus of my life, so that I magnify You. Give me courage to deal with idols and high places that I have tolerated but never removed. Let me restore Your altar in my life (v. 8).

I want to live in covenant with You. Teach me to seek You deliberately with all my heart and soul (v. 12). Show me any area where my heart is divided. I want to obey You. I want to glorify You. Let my soul long after You (v. 15). Father, send revival among Your people. In Jesus' name, amen.

Reflection Questions

1. The fear of God means loving what God loves and hating what God hates. God loves wisdom (Proverbs 2:1–2, 5–6), and hates evil and sin. How does your life demonstrate the fear of God?

2. The fear of God shows itself when we understand who God is and have correct concepts of God's character. How does your

life demonstrate His character?

3. Our personal obligation to God is to love Him supremely, obey Him explicitly, and trust Him completely. How do you demonstrate these things?

4. When we are overly attached to things of the world and are less attached to things of God, we demonstrate a lack of the fear of God. What things in your life show a lack of fear and respect for who God is?

Chapter 7

REVIVAL under JEHOSHAPHAT: Seeking God

Then you will call upon Me and go and pray to Me, and I will listen to you. And you will seek Me and find Me, when you search for Me with all your heart. I will be found by you, says the LORD. (JEREMIAH 29:12–14)

SCRIPTURE:
2 CHRONICLES 20:1–4, 6–7, 9, 13–15, 17–18

It happened after this *that* the people of Moab with the people of Ammon, and *others* with them beside the Ammonites, came to battle against Jehoshaphat. Then some came and told Jehoshaphat, saying, "A great multitude is coming against you" . . . And Jehoshaphat feared, and set himself to seek the LORD, and proclaimed a fast throughout all Judah. So Judah gathered together to ask *help* from the LORD; and from all the cities of Judah they came to seek the LORD. Then Jehoshaphat . . . said, "O LORD God of our fathers, *are* You not God in heaven, and do You *not* rule over all the kingdoms of the nations, and in Your hand *is there not* power and might, so that no one is able to withstand You? *Are* You not our God, *who* drove out the inhabitants of this land before Your people Israel, and gave it to the descendants of Abraham Your friend forever? 'If disaster comes upon us—sword, judgment, pestilence, or famine—we will stand before this temple and in Your presence (for Your name *is* in this temple), and cry out to You in our affliction, and You will hear and save.'"

Now all Judah . . . stood before the LORD.

Then the Spirit of the LORD came upon Jahaziel the son of Zechariah. . . . "Thus says the LORD to you: 'Do not be afraid nor dismayed because of this great multitude, for the battle *is* not yours but God's. . . . You will not *need* to fight in this *battle.* Position yourselves, stand still and see the salvation of the LORD, who is with you, O Judah and Jerusalem!' Do not fear or be dismayed; tomorrow go out against them, for the LORD *is* with you."

And Jehoshaphat bowed his head with *his* face to the ground, and all of Judah and the inhabitants of Jerusalem bowed before the LORD, worshiping the LORD.

Seeking God

It takes practice to become good at anything, and we must practice pursuing God's presence, seeking Him every day until pursuing Him becomes the norm for our lives. Seeking God is a key in revival times.

It would do us all good to pause and examine our lives, seeing what we really spend our time seeking after. J. Vernon McGee said, "What is your ambition in life today? Is it to get rich? Is it to make a name for yourself? Is it even to do some wonderful thing for God? Listen to me, beloved. The highest desire that can possess any human heart is a longing to see God."[10]

Many people seek the wrong things and then want to add God

to the end of their list. People seek comfort and convenience, but not Christ. They seek pleasure and pastimes, but not a personal relationship with Christ. Most people look for a church that has the right appeal: good music and children's and youth programs. They seek the church with all the answers to their problems or needs. For many, they confuse this with seeking God; this is not the same thing.

Many have been led to believe they can seek God at their own convenience, but you cannot. Many a professing believer has been hurt, or gotten angry with the church or God, and left. Others have remained in the church but are filled with bitterness. They refuse to examine their lives in light of the Word of God, nor do they yield to the Word of God. Instead of turning to God, they have turned away. After weeks, months, or even years of not seeking God, a crisis comes, an emergency, and then they expect a dead faith to work in their time of need.[11] It does not happen.

D. L. Moody said, "We ought to see the face of God every morning before we see the face of man."[12]

In this section of Scripture, we find Jehoshaphat and all Judah under attack from the world, the people of Moab and Ammon. Jehoshaphat was outnumbered and all looked hopeless. He was afraid. Faith does not keep us from fear, but enables us to seek God in spite of our fears. Jehoshaphat sought God.

To seek God simply means we pursue God. He is preeminent. That means He is not merely a priority, but everything is around Him. When we seek God, we desire more than anything the "face" of God, His presence. We desire intimacy with Him more than anything else. Our lifestyle is that of pursuing, learning about, and communing with God. It takes time, energy, even resources to seek God.

We are commanded in Scripture (Jeremiah 29:12–14) to seek Him diligently and with urgency.

When we seek God, we are volunteering ourselves for judgment. We have reached a point in our lives where we are willing to be honest with the Word of God and how we live. It means we humble ourselves before God and also the one whom God uses to bring the message of the Word of God to us. Then, we adjust our lives to God's standards.

Having the Right Attitude

Our attitude determines if we receive God's Word or not. According to James 1:21, we are to have an attitude of meekness to receive the implanted (engrafted) Word of God. All of this is a result of our having a hunger for the approval of God more than the approval of humans.

Jehoshaphat put aside everything in order to seek God. This was not a spur of the moment decision. We see in 2 Chronicles 19:3, he had removed the wooden images and prepared his heart to seek God. He did this before the invading army showed up to battle against him. American evangelist R. A. Torrey, who was a contemporary of D. L. Moody, said: "The reason many fail in battle is because they wait until the hour of battle. The reason why others succeed is because they have gained their victory on their knees long before the battle came. . . . Anticipate your battles; fight them on your knees before temptation comes, and you will always have victory."[13] Jehoshaphat succeeded in battle because he had already positioned himself to seek God. Likewise, we must remove from our hearts and lives anything that is offensive to God and distracts us from Him. Then we can fully seek God on our knees.

Getting Personal

The Tennessee revival meetings were scheduled to begin on October 13, a Sunday morning. Prior to the meeting time, we had times of prayer and corporate confession of sin. In these meetings, we experienced a fresh cleansing from God. We thought we were ready spiritually. How far from the truth that was!

We planned the services, we did all that we were supposed to do to have a good series of revival meetings. God, however, had other plans. We were not ready. The day before the meetings began, our revivalist received an urgent call: "Come home. A dear friend and church member, the sheriff, has been killed in the line of duty." We postponed our meeting so this urgent need could be met. We had our Sunday morning and evening meeting, and our revivalist left to minister to this family and hold the funeral service.

That Monday, we called for another prayer meeting. We planned to meet every night till the revivalist was able to return the next weekend. Laymen would lead the meetings. On the first Monday, less than twenty people came out to pray, and prayer was difficult. We seemed just to go through the motions. We went home unchanged. By the last night, the man who led the prayer cried out to God with an urgency that had not been expressed before. He talked about how it was no mistake that the revival was postponed because our hearts were unprepared. He prayed, "God, it is time we get serious and we stop playing games. It is time we get serious about our lives. Oh, God, we seek You, we need You."

As the people lay with their faces on the altar, the fervency of prayer began to build. People repented of their attitudes and asked God to move like we had never seen before. At some point we crossed over to God's agenda.

We did not stop seeking God. Early the following Monday morning, people began coming to the church to pray and seek the Lord. At lunchtime, new people came from their workplaces and sought the Lord. Before the services started, people came early to pray and seek the Lord. There was a sense of holy reverence. There was no socializing, talking, or visiting. No one asked these people to come; they were led by the Father, drawn by His Holy Spirit, to seek His face and cry out for revival. They continued to come week after week, seeking God.

Additional Scripture on Seeking God

Deuteronomy 4:29; 1 Chronicles 16:11; 2 Chronicles 19:3; Psalm 105:3; Isaiah 51:1; Hosea 7:10; Acts 17:27

Scriptural Prayer for Revival

Gracious Father, to the degree I seek You will be the degree I experience You. Send revival. I need You, and I seek You with all my strength and might. Let me be constantly aware of a world that opposes You and Your people (2 Chronicles 20:1). Amidst all the challenges of the world, show me the importance of seeking You (v. 2).

Father, let me understand when fear rises in my heart, it is a call to seek You. Thank You for Your promises, protection, and provision. Teach me dependency on You. In the face of adversity, teach me to seek You first and always. Drive me to my knees. Just as Jehoshaphat called a fast, Father, allow me to know when to fast individually and when to call a corporate fast (v. 3).

Father, I volunteer for Your Word to judge me. Show me myself in light of Your Word. Use Your preacher, whomever You choose, to proclaim Your Word to me. Let meekness be my attitude, so I can receive Your Word. Let me yield to Your Word. I ask Your help (vv. 4,

14). Lord, teach me to ask You for help, but do not let pride prevent me from allowing people to help me if You choose to work through them (v. 4).

Show me those things that distract me from You, and allow me by faith to yield them to You. You are a mighty God. You are all powerful. You are sovereign. You are in control of everything. Thank You for Your mighty acts on my behalf and on behalf of Your people. Thank You for Your Word. Thank You for the Holy Spirit. Thank You for Your deliverance (vv. 6–7).

Oh, Lord, teach me to fear You. Even in a disaster, let me seek You; let me not forsake the church, the body of Christ (v. 9). Let Your church stand before You, just as Jehoshaphat did. Let us stand before You, so we also can hear You and know Your truth (v. 13).

Fill me with Your Holy Spirit, as I yield myself to You. Keep me sensitive to Your Spirit, for Your glory, not mine. Increase my faith and understanding of Your Word. Amidst opposition and turmoil, let me be still so I can hear Your voice (vv. 14–15). Teach me, Lord, what it means to position myself in You, and let me claim Your promise (v. 17).

I bless Your name. I praise You. Lord, I seek You. I bow before You, not just at church, but throughout the day. Let me bow before You, even in front of others, because You are my God. Let me worship You (v. 18). Send revival, and let it begin in me. In Jesus' name, amen.

Reflection Questions

1. Have you prepared your heart to seek God? How, specifically?
2. Do you have any commitments to the world that keep you from seeking God? If so, what are they? Talk to God about these now.

3. Are you experiencing any opposition or crisis right now? If so, what? How could God be using these to get you to seek Him?

4. We are called to seek God with diligence. What would diligence in your crisis look like?

5. Seeking God will transform your prayer life. What evidence is there that your prayer life is being transformed?

Chapter 8

REVIVAL under ELIJAH: Repairing the Altar

Oh, send out Your light and Your truth! Let them lead me; Let them bring me to Your holy hill And to Your tabernacle. Then I will go to the altar of God, To God my exceeding joy; And on the harp I will praise You, O God, my God. (PSALM 43:3–4)

SCRIPTURE:
1 KINGS 17:1–4; 18:1–2, 30–33, 36–39

And Elijah the Tishbite, of the inhabitants of Gilead, said to Ahab, "As the LORD of Israel lives, before whom I stand, there shall not be dew nor rain these years except at my word."

Then the word of the LORD came to him, saying, "Get away from here and turn eastward, and hide by the Brook Cherith, which flows into the Jordan. And it will be *that* you shall drink from the brook, and I have commanded the ravens to feed you there." . . .

And it came to pass *after* many days that the word of the LORD came to Elijah, in the third year, saying, "Go, present yourself to Ahab, and I will send rain on the earth."

So Elijah went and presented himself to Ahab; and *there was* a severe famine in Samaria. . . .

Then Elijah said to all the people, "Come near to me." So all the people came near to him. And he repaired the altar of the LORD *that was* broken down. And Elijah took twelve stones, according to the number of the tribes of the sons of Jacob, to whom the word of the LORD had come, saying, "Israel shall be your name." Then with the stones he built an altar in the name of the LORD; and he made a trench around the altar large enough to hold two seahs of seed. And he put the wood in order, cut the bull in pieces, and laid *it* on the wood, and said, "Fill four water pots with water, and pour *it* on the burnt sacrifice and on the wood.". . .

Elijah the prophet came near and said, "LORD God of Abraham, Isaac, and Israel, let it be known this day that You *are* God in Israel and I *am* Your servant, and *that* I have done all these things at Your word. Hear me, O LORD, hear me, that this people may know that You *are* the LORD God, and *that* You have turned their hearts back *to You* again."

Then the fire of the LORD fell and consumed the burnt sacrifice, and the wood and the stones and the dust, and it licked up the water that *was* in the trench. Now when all the people *saw it,* they fell on their faces; and they said, "The LORD, He *is* God! The LORD, He *is* God!"

Repairing the Broken Altar

"Several decades ago, scientists made a discovery. They found that if they took a wooden door and encased it in copper so that it was perfectly sealed that the door literally became fireproof. Wood won't burn when it is encased in certain metals . . . like bronze (an alloy usually made of copper and tin)."[14]

When Jesus died at Calvary, on what did He die? A cross made of wood. The only altar in Scripture that was made of wood was the cross. The blood of Jesus Christ was offered to God on the altar of redemption, the cross.

The Hebrew word for "altar" means "the place of putting to death, as a sacrifice." It is a place of sacrifice and surrender. An altar is a place where we approach God. In the Bible, we find altars made of stone, earth, and even metal. It matters not the material; what matters is how the altar is used.

In Leviticus 8:11, Moses anointed the altar with oil seven times. Next, he sacrificed a sin offering, pouring the blood upon and around the altar, purifying and consecrating the altar (vv. 14–15). Finally, he offered burnt offerings and sprinkled blood on the altar (vv. 18–19). Why did he do all this? He was following God's command, because the altar had to be prepared and made holy. "Seven days you shall make atonement for the altar and sanctify it. And the altar shall be most holy. Whatever touches the altar must be holy" (Exodus 29:37). The altar was made holy by being anointed with blood, and was so holy that anything placed on it was also sanctified or made holy.

Although believers no longer make animal sacrifices on an altar, Hebrews 13:10 tells us, "We have an altar." It is the altar where the Son of God, the Lamb, was sacrificed. That altar is the cross. When Jesus Christ died on the cross, His blood was shed and the cross was sanctified by His blood. Today, that altar has the power through Christ to make us holy. But to receive that power, we must come to the altar and abide there. "I beseech you therefore, by the mercies of God, that you present your bodies a living sacrifice, holy, acceptable unto God, which is your reasonable service" (Romans 12:1).

How does an altar get broken? Altars get broken by neglect and lack of use. Clearly, we can do nothing to diminish the work of the cross. It is perfect, never needing repair. We have to learn, however, to run to the altar and to appropriate it by faith. We have to learn that the altar is the place of abiding. The only way we can repair the altar is by repairing the *use* of the altar.

Elijah "repaired the altar of the LORD that was broken down." The Hebrew word translated "repaired" means to "heal" or "to restore." It is used in the context of healing the hurt of a nation and regaining God's favor. The people of God had allowed their relationship with God to diminish so much that the altar had been neglected. Elijah acknowledged the sin and interceded on behalf of the people, and God answered with fire.

Oftentimes in our personal lives, we neglect the altar of our heart and it grows dilapidated and broken. We fail to abide in Christ. Without the altar, we have no place to receive the forgiveness of sin or to bring our sacrifices. To repair the altar, we must come to Christ, acknowledging our need and petitioning God for our lives, begging His forgiveness as we confess and repent of our sins. Thus, our altar is repaired as we once again seek to abide daily in Christ. In revival, the altar of our heart is of foremost importance.

Preparing for Usefulness

Scripture tells us that Elijah was a man with the same nature that we have (James 5:17). He came out of obscurity (he had been hidden away) and then stood before the world powers of his day, pronouncing God's judgment on them. This is never a popular message. If your desire is to be popular, you will never be used by God.

Before he was used by God to repair the altar of a wayward people, Elijah was hidden away for three years. What does the hidden-away life mean? Matthew 6:28 tells us to consider the lilies, see how they grow; they neither toil nor spin. The lily spends most of its life hidden away in the ground, drawing its strength from its environment, abiding. Elijah was hidden away so he could abide in God and later become useful. Likewise, our hidden away time is to be spent abiding in the presence of God, drawing our strength from our environment, Jesus Christ. Welsh minister Seth Joshua talked about prayer and being hidden away: "All prayer is hidden. It is behind a closed door. The best spade diggers go down into the deep ditches out of sight. There are a number of surface workers, but few in self-obliteration toil alone with God."[15]

Elijah lived his life in obedience to God, to God's Word, to God's direction. He lived depending on God's provision to sustain him in the wilderness. Elijah returned in the power of the Lord after three years of being hidden away. He challenged the people of God to stop wavering between two opinions, and if God be God, serve Him. If Baal be the true god, serve him. He then began to repair the altar of the Lord that was broken down on Mt. Carmel.

Before God will move in any of our lives, our personal altars must be repaired. The fire of God will fall only on a prepared altar, on a prepared heart. When the fire fell on the altar, God's people proclaimed God as the true God. An altar is a place you meet with God and surrender to God. It is a place to offer sacrifice to God. Do you need to repair your personal altar?

Getting Personal

Several years ago, I was in Ireland preaching at a small revival conference. The participants and I were in a conference room of a nice hotel, and the host pastor introduced me to a couple who had traveled about two hours to attend. They seemed pleasant and sincere.

Toward the end of the service, I said, "You may need to go to the altar and seek God. Seek God's forgiveness and cleansing." Nothing unusual in the appeal. I even said they could stay where they were and that their seat could be an altar, but that they needed to talk with God.

After the service ended, this pleasant couple came to me and said, "The idea of an altar is grotesque. The concept of blood and sacrifice is unpleasant."

I was dumbfounded. I explained that God established the altar and that Jesus died as a substitute for us on the cross. He bore our sin and shame. He took our penalty that we may approach God.

In response, they simply walked away.

I asked the host pastor if I had said or done something wrong. He said, "No." I relayed what had just occurred, and he was amazed.

Clearly, here was a couple who needed to repair the broken altar of their hearts and meet with God, but they refused.

In churches in the South, we southerners refer to the place in front of the pulpit area as the altar. It is a place where we come for prayer. In another revival conference, I noticed the sanctuary of the church had no altar area, no place for a person to respond by coming forward to pray. Between the elevated pulpit and the first row of pews was only a small walkway. I understand you do not have to come forward, but there are times everyone needs the opportunity to respond publically. It may not be our tradition to come forward, nor is it always necessary. Perhaps, though, we have no expectancy for God to move in our midst as we are called to respond publicly.

One thing is certain: We all need an altar, both private and public. We have to maintain our altars or they will disappear. When revival comes, the altar is where God's fire will fall.

Additional Scripture on Repairing the Altar

Genesis 22:9; 2 Chronicles 8:12, 29:18, 33:16; Ezra 3:2–3; Joel 2:17

Scriptural Prayer for Revival

Holy Father, send revival on the altar of my life. Oh, how the altar needs to be restored in me and in Your church. Let me accept Your Word, even if it is confrontational and challenging. Lord, let me be bold in proclaiming Your Word (1 Kings 17:1).

Lord, You spoke to Elijah and he recognized Your voice. Let me recognize Your voice, Your Word when it comes to me (v. 2).

Teach me the importance of following Your leadership and trusting You for my provision. Even when You take me to wilderness experiences, let me trust You (vv. 3–4).

Father, I come before You asking for a fresh Word; Your Word is truth. Show me if I have failed to adjust my life to any previous Word You have given, and let me do so now (18:1).

Just as You did with Elijah, enable me by Your Holy Spirit to hear You when You speak. Give me faith to obey Your Word, even if I think it does not make sense. May I understand that You orchestrate famines—financial famines, relational famines, physical famines—to teach me to trust You. In seasons of famine and need, teach me to depend on You and Your Word, letting me respond quickly to Your Word (v. 2).

Lord, let me maintain Your altar so it does not become neglected. But if it does become broken, teach me how to repair and restore the altar (v. 30).

Show me how to prepare and bring sacrifices that are pleasing to You. Show me how to adjust my life to You and Your commands (v. 33).

Let me pray with boldness. Give me opportunities to share my testimony with a watching world. Let me fill my mind with Your Word, so I can resist Satan's lies and deception (vv. 36–37). Answer my prayer God, as I repair the altar for Your glory. As the world dances and frolics to Satan's lies, let me obey You. Capture my heart, my mind, my all for Your kingdom. Let me make a sacrifice that is truly sacrificial. Lord, let Your fire fall on this place, on this altar. Consume everything that is of this world and of the flesh (v. 38).

Father, let a watching church, Your people, see and respond to You. Let us fall on our face before You and proclaim, "The Lord, He is God," just as Israel did (v. 39).

Oh, God, I am desperate for revival. Let the altar flood with broken people sacrificing unto You, rebuilding personal altars as they return to You. In Jesus' name, amen.

Reflection Questions

1. Do you have a regular place to seek God and pray? If so, where and when do you go?

2. Neglected altars become flawed and broken. How has sin interrupted your time with God in prayer?

3. To repair the altar, we must give attention to our relationship with Jesus Christ by returning to the place (going back) where we met God. We must come with honest confession, obedience, and repentance from the things that took us away. We must adjust our lives to God, God's Word, and God's people. What steps have you taken to accomplish this?

4. Has the fire of God fallen on the sacrifice you have made on the repaired altar? If not, why not?

Chapter 9

REVIVAL under HEZEKIAH: Continuing Sanctification

Elect according to the foreknowledge of God the Father,
in sanctification of the Spirit, for obedience and sprinkling
of the blood of Jesus Christ: Grace to you and peace
be multiplied. (1 PETER 1:2)

SCRIPTURE:
2 CHRONICLES 30:1, 6–12, 15–16, 18–19, 27

And Hezekiah sent to all Israel and Judah, and also wrote letters to Ephraim and Manasseh, that they should come to the house of the LORD at Jerusalem, to keep the Passover to the LORD God of Israel. . . .

Runners . . . spoke according to the command of the king: "Children of Israel, return to the LORD God of Abraham, Isaac, and Israel; then He will return to the remnant of you who have escaped from the hand of the kings of Assyria. And do not be like your fathers and brethren, who trespassed against the LORD God of their fathers, so that He gave them up to desolation, as you see. Now do not be stiff-necked, as your fathers *were*, *but* yield yourself to the LORD; and enter His sanctuary, which He has sanctified forever, and serve the LORD your God, that the fierceness of

His wrath may turn away from you. For if you return to the LORD, your brethren and your children *will be treated* with compassion by those who lead them captive, so that they may come back to this land; for the LORD your God *is* gracious and merciful, and will not turn *His* face from you if you return to Him."

So the runners passed from city to city through the country of Ephraim and Manasseh, as far as Zebulun; but they laughed at them and mocked them. Nevertheless some from Asher, Manasseh, and Zebulun humbled themselves and came to Jerusalem. Also the hand of God was on Judah to give them singleness of heart to obey the command of the king and the leaders, at the word of the LORD. . . .

The priests and Levites were ashamed, and sanctified themselves, and brought burnt offerings to the house of the LORD. They stood in their place according to their custom, according to the Law of Moses the man of God; the priests sprinkled the blood *received* from the hand of the Levites. . . .

Hezekiah prayed for [the unsanctified multitudes], saying, "May the good LORD provide atonement for everyone *who* prepares his heart to seek God. . . ."

Then the priests, the Levites, arose and blessed the people, and their voice was heard; and their prayer came *up* to His holy dwelling place, to heaven.

Continuing Sanctification

Some time ago, *Our Daily Bread* devotional carried this concise description of the need for continuing sanctification: "When a person becomes a Christian, he usually undergoes some radical life changes, especially if he has had an immoral background. Through the first steps of spiritual growth and self-denial, he gets rid of the large, obvious sins. But sad to say, many believers stop there. They don't go on to eliminate the little sins that clutter the landscape of their lives."[16]

In his book *Ordering Your Private World*, Gordon MacDonald related a personal experience that illustrates this same truth: "Some years ago, when Gail and I bought the old abandoned New Hampshire farm we now call Peace Ledge, we found the site where we wished to build our country home strewn with rocks and boulders. It was going to take a lot of hard work to clear it all out. . . . The first phase of the clearing process was easy. The big boulders went fast. And when they were gone, we began to see that there were a lot of smaller rocks that had to go, too. But when we had cleared the site of the boulders and the rocks, we noticed all of the stones and pebbles we had not seen before. This was much harder, more tedious work. But we stuck to it, and there came the day when the soil was ready for planting grass."[17]

Sanctification means "to be set apart." It is the process after salvation where we are made into the image of Christ Jesus. God sanctifies us by faith (Acts 26:18) and truth (John 17:19). Our part is to yield ourselves, after salvation, to God. God will not force Himself on anyone, saved or lost. We are to submit ourselves willingly to the Word of God. Just as repentance and faith involve our emotions, intellect, and will, in sanctification these are also involved. We are enabled to die to sin more and more, and we live unto the glory of God and His righteousness.

Every day, the power of sin is diminished as we live by the principles of God's Word. The Holy Spirit begins to control our thoughts, feelings, and acts. We are brought into conformity with the image of Christ. This does not happen instantly, but rather day by day as we yield to Him. Our minds are transformed, our emotions are changed, and our desire for God grows stronger. Through our sanctified will, we rid our lives of boulders of unrighteousness and pebbles of sin. Our responsibility is to cooperate with God, and God provides the power for our sanctification. In times of revival, our sanctification will be visible.

Revival always brings a church to its knees. Hezekiah was twenty-five years old when he came to the throne. He was raised by a godless father in a godless age. Godlessness means there is no time for God. Much of America has no time for God. Even many who profess Christ have no time for Him. To assess yourself, all you have to do is compare how much time you spend communing with God in prayer and Bible study compared to time spent watching television, being online or on Facebook, and so forth. There are 168 hours in a week. How much time do we give to God? Do we give only one to two hours on a Sunday? That is about 1.25 percent. Does that amount of time qualify it as important?

Reaching Hidden Areas

Hezekiah had not been equipped by his father to serve the Lord; yet, the text tells us "he did what was right in the sight of the LORD" (2 Chronicles 29:2). The first act Hezekiah did as king was to open the doors of the house of the Lord and repair them. Repairs began with what everyone could see, and moved into the place only God and the priest would see. Priests began removing all the rubbish and trash, cleansing the sanctuary of God.

It is never enough merely to deal with those areas that human eyes can see—the outer court. We must always go to the area only God sees and knows, hidden from the human eyes. These areas are crucial to our being right with God and to experience revival. Evangelist

Wellington Boone said: "When men fall on their knees and cry out to God, that's where true intimacy with God takes place and we begin the journey of being transformed into the image of Christ. And as men are transformed, the course of a nation can be changed."[18]

When cleansing takes place in our lives and the proper purpose of life has been reestablished, the Scripture calls that sanctification.

Getting Personal

When I was a pastor in West Virginia, I met a man named Jack who told me how he came to faith in Jesus Christ. A man at his workplace lived his faith in front of him and witnessed to him. This impacted Jack to the point that he gave his life to Christ. Jack came to church and publically acknowledged what Christ had done for him, and he was baptized.

What Jack told me next was so encouraging. He said, "I did not know what to do next? How was I to grow as a Christian, or how was I to mature in my faith? I decided whatever they did at church, I was going to be a part. Whatever they asked me to do, I would do. I would read my Bible and pray. I would daily have my devotions. I would attend Bible study, prayer meetings, and fellowships. I would do this for one year, and at the end of one year, if my life had not changed, then I would stop."

Needless to say, Jack never stopped. At the end of one year, his life had so radically changed that he never wanted to stop. He responded to the Word of God and to the body of Christ, and he grew into a mature believer.

Narrowing Our Lives

Sanctification is God narrowing your life to His, and you never want to stop. The mistake many people seem to make is they try to add the things of God to their lives, while at the same time trying to retain the things of this world. To put on Christ Jesus, we must take off the things of this world. We cannot live in both worlds.

In times of revival, I watched as God narrowed my own life to His. No longer did I desire to spend my time in trivial things, such as television, the Internet, or even sport scores. My consuming desire was Christ. For weeks, I never watched the news or read a newspaper; all that mattered was Christ. I found I did not have to *try not* to do these things; I simply lost all desire for them.

In the Old Testament, one of the names for God is Jehovah-M'Kaddesh (Exodus 31:13), meaning "the Lord who sanctifies." We are told in Joshua 1:8, "This Book of the Law shall not depart from your mouth, but you shall meditate in it day and night, that you may observe to do according to all that is written in it. For then you will make your way prosperous, and then you will have good success." If we want to be successful in our walk with God, in our life, we are told how. Meditate on the Scriptures. Give thought to the Word of God. Roll it over in your mind and process the truth of God. Meditate and obey it. Adjust your life to the Bible. It is through this process that sanctification comes and we know success. We know how to live the right path. God sanctifies and in seasons of revival He sanctifies us intensely as we respond to His truth by faith.

Additional Scripture on Sanctification

John 17:17; Ephesians 5:25–26; 1 Thessalonians 4:3; Hebrews 13:20–21

Scriptural Prayer for Revival

Merciful Father, Your Word is truth and sanctifies me with truth.

Please sanctify Your people with truth. I pray You will burn Your Word in my heart and mind, so I can know Scripture and be an effective witness. Show me how to encourage others to come to Your house, the church, just as Hezekiah did (2 Chronicles 30:1).

Show me those times I have failed to be in church with Your people as You desire, and narrow my life to You. Do I treat the observance of the Lord's Supper as common? Do I miss this observance and think it is no big deal? (v. 1).

Father, when You tell me to return, that means I must have gone away and am backslidden. Let me be sensitive to Your calling to return. Show me my heart. Does it burn for You and Your kingdom? Show me my priorities as they really are (v. 6).

Teach me not to be stiff-necked and stubborn, but yielded to You. Bend me and mold me into Your image, and give me a passion for Your presence. Teach me repentance. Teach me to learn that the place of humility is the place of blessing, power, and joy. Teach me submission to You, to Your Word. Teach me what it truly means to yield to You (vv. 7–8).

Father, teach me the importance and necessity of coming to Your sanctuary. Show me how I am to be serving You (v. 8).

Lord, let me seek Your face and find it. Please do not turn away from me (v. 9). When men laugh and mock me, Father, enable me still to be faithful to You (v. 10). Teach me to humble myself unto You. Let me understand that the world will laugh and scorn me, but let me be faithful (v. 11).

Give me singleness of heart for You. Let me know where I should truly give my attention. Show me if I have made an idol of my family, friends, entertainment, or my job. Let me obey Your Word (v. 12).

Father, teach me the steps I must take in the sanctification process.

Teach me to bring an acceptable offering to You. Teach me the importance of time with You daily in Your Word, in prayer, in acts of service, and in proclaiming You to others. Show me those things I must put out of my life (v. 15).

Father, let me be found in my place of responsibility. Let me apply the blood of Christ to my life (v. 16). Forgive my sin, and let me have clean hands and a pure heart. Let me be clean inwardly and outwardly, so I may be an intercessor for the body of Christ (vv. 18–19). Lord, as Hezekiah instructed the people to prepare their hearts, let me prepare my heart to seek You (v. 19).

Oh, Father, let me be faithful to intercede for Your people, and let my prayers reach Your presence (v. 27). We need revival, so send it now. Sanctify me in truth, fill me with Your joy, and let me abide in Your presence. Give me understanding and knowledge of You. I praise You and exalt You, my God. Help me to adjust my life to Your Word and will. Sanctify me, oh, God. In Jesus' name, amen.

Reflection Questions

1. Sanctification will not take place as long as we allow rivals for our time, talents, and treasures. What things do you allow to compete for your time and talents?

2. Of the 168 hours in a week, how much time do you spend seeking and communing with God? Do you tithe your time? For instance, 16.8 hours a week, or 2.4 hours a day?

3. How would giving the Word of God and prayer top priority affect your life day by day? How will you know you are giving God's Word top priority?

4. As we yield to the Holy Spirit, He sanctifies us. How do you yield to the Holy Spirit? What does that look like?

Chapter 10

REVIVAL under JOSIAH:
Rediscovering the Word of God

*For the word of God is living and powerful, and sharper than
any two-edged sword, piercing even to the division of soul
and spirit, and of joints and marrow, and is a discerner of
the thoughts and intents of the heart.* (HEBREWS 4:12)

SCRIPTURE:
2 CHRONICLES 34:1–3, 8, 14–16, 18–19, 21, 26–27, 30–31, 33

Josiah was eight years old when he became king, and he reigned
thirty-one years in Jerusalem. And he did *what was* right in the
sight of the LORD, and walked in the ways of his father David; *he*
did *not* turn aside to the right hand or to the left.

For in the eighth year of his reign, while he was still young,
he began to seek the God of his father David; and in the twelfth
year he began to purge Judah and Jerusalem of the high places,
the wooden images, the carved images, and the molded images.

In the eighteenth year of his reign, when he had purged the
land and the temple, he sent Shaphan the son of Azaliah, Maaseiah the governor of the city, and Joah the son of Joahaz the
recorder, to repair the house of the LORD his God. . . .

Hilkiah the priest found the Book of the Law of the LORD *given* by Moses. Then Hilkiah answered and said to Shaphan the scribe, "I have found the Book of the Law in the house of the LORD." And Hilkiah gave the book to Shaphan. So Shaphan carried the book to the king, bringing the king word, saying, "All that was committed to your servant they are doing. . . ." Then Shaphan the scribe told the king, saying, "Hilkiah the priest has given me a book." And Shaphan read it before the king.

Thus it happened, when the king heard the words of the Law, that the king tore his clothes. . . [saying] "Go, inquire of the LORD for me, and for those who are left in Israel and Judah, concerning the words of the book that is found; for great *is* the wrath of the LORD that is poured out on us, because our fathers have not kept the word of the LORD, to do according to all that is written in this book.". . .

"'Thus says the LORD God of Israel: "*Concerning* the words which you have heard—because your heart was tender, and you humbled yourself before God when you heard His words against this place and against its inhabitants, and you humbled yourself before Me, and you tore your clothes and wept before Me, I also have heard *you*," says the LORD.'"

The king went up to the house of the LORD, with all the men of Judah. . . . And he read in their hearing all the words in the Book of the Covenant which had been found in the house of the LORD. Then the king stood in his place and made a covenant before the LORD, and to follow the LORD, and to keep His commandments and His testimonies and His statutes with all his heart and all his soul, to perform the words of the covenant that were written in this book. . . . Thus Josiah removed all the abominations from all the country that *belonged* to the children of Israel, and made all who were present in Israel diligently serve the LORD their God. All his days they did not depart from following the LORD God of their fathers.

Rediscovering the Word of God

The Bible is the best-selling book in the history of the world, and our world is saturated with Bibles. I believe there are more than 250 translations. In a real sense, however, the Bible needs to be rediscovered. "Rediscovered" suggests that something has been lost, misplaced, or neglected, and now has been found.

The Word of God is precious, and we must meditate on it every day and draw our strength from it. Nevertheless, there will be times when we will read it and think we have not gained any new understanding or insight. Yet when we face a decision, our minds will be prompted by the Word of God on what to do.

The Word of God is infallible and inerrant, but these things mean little unless the Word of God is sufficient to us: sufficient to live by, sufficient to lean on, sufficient to trust. The sufficiency of the Word is seen when we apply it to our lives. Have you experienced the Word of God as sufficient?

In revival, the Word of God is primary. It is through God's Word, preached and taught, that God speaks His will and way to us. But then, we must respond in obedience by adjusting our lives to the Word of God.

Josiah found himself in the position of king at the early age of eight. This was not by choice, but by default. His father Ammon was an evil king, as was his grandfather Manasseh. Ammon was so evil the people assassinated him. This left his son, an eight-year-old boy as king. If he was overwhelmed, it never showed.

The timeline of Josiah's life is powerful. At age eight, he became king. He reigned thirty-one years, and despite Josiah's poor heritage and sinful home environment, lacking good role models, he did what was right in the sight of the Lord. At age sixteen, he began to seek God. When he was twenty, he began to rid the land of false idols and idol worship. Finally, at twenty-six years of age, after he had purged the land and the temple, he found the Book of the Law, Israel's Bible at that time. As he heard its words, his heart broke and he repented in sackcloth and ashes. He urged the people under his rule to turn back to God, and he had the Book of the Law read aloud to all those in his territory.

How far away from God had his nation gone? They had lost focus on the one true God and had substituted their own gods in His place. They were going through the religious motions, but not meeting God. They were so far away that they did not even realize their Bible was missing, let alone know what it said!

Josiah's life proves that God can use a person of any age. God's Word is relevant, sufficient, and precious to all people of all ages.

Oh, how we need to rediscover the Word of God, but do we recognize our need? Have we become satisfied with other things? Oswald Chambers said, "A great many people do not pray because they do not feel any sense of need. The sign that the Holy Spirit is in us is that we realize we are empty, not that we are full. We have a sense of absolute need. . . . If we are ever free from the sense of need, it is not because the Holy Spirit has satisfied us, but because we have been satisfied with as much as we have."[19]

Ole S. Hallesby, a Norwegian pietist and outspoken critic of the Nazi occupation of Norway, said much the same thing, "To strive in prayer means to struggle through those hindrances which would restrain or even prevent us entirely from continuing in persevering prayer. It means to be so watchful at all times that we can notice when we become slothful in prayer and go to the Spirit of prayer to have this remedied."[20]

God's Word shows us how much we need. We must read, absorb, apply, and obey it. We are responsible for radically adjusting our lives to truth, the Word of God, just as Josiah did.

Getting Personal

Matthew showed up for church one Sunday night about two weeks after the start of the continuous revival meetings where I was ministering. He had not been to the church in six or seven years, and he was now twenty-three years old. As he left, I thought, *I wonder when I will see him again. Probably at a funeral.* To my surprise, he came back to church one Sunday morning a few weeks later. He sat in the back, and when the service ended, he left.

The next week, I was in my study. Guess who showed up? Matthew. We talked awhile about general things, and then we moved into some more serious issues—his walk with God and his relationship to the church. The next Sunday, he was back in church, and that week he showed up in my office again. After general talk, he asked, "Do you think I am saved?"

I told him as gently as I knew how that he showed no evidence of being born again. There was no fruit in his life.

He left, came back to church the following Sunday, and was back in my office the next week to talk. He told me later the reason he kept coming back was that I was honest with him. "You had something I didn't have," he said, "and I wanted it." I had assurance of salvation.

Matthew continued seeking God as best he knew how. He continued to respond to the light that he had, and God gave him more light. Ultimately, Matthew was born again. When he showed up in my office, he was smiling ear to ear. He could not stop smiling. Matthew had met Jesus Christ in a real and personal way. He knew he was saved.

From that day on, it appeared Matthew always had a Bible in his possession. He carried it everywhere, reading it over and over. He stopped by my office to ask me questions about the Scriptures. He would ask, "Well, Preacher, what's God been saying to you this week?"

The Bible became the Word of eternal life to him. It is fresh and exciting for him. His hunger for Scripture is ferocious, and he continues to have that big smile on his face.

Additional Scripture on Rediscovering the Word of God

Proverbs 30:5; Luke 4:4; 8:21; Acts 4:31, 12:24

Scriptural Prayer for Revival

Precious Father, Your Word is the living Word. Your Word desperately needs to be rediscovered in Your church. Father, I want to walk in Your ways and be a person of God. Show me what that involves. Show me how to pursue You, and how to separate myself from the world (2 Chronicles 34:1–2).

Teach me the importance of seeking You, even in my youth as Josiah did, and let me instill that to my children (v. 3).

Father, let me be an instrument of purging my land of false idols. Let me recognize them as they deceive and pull people away from You. Let me recognize how Your church needs Your purging from complacency and compromise. Purge my sin (v. 8). And let me be able to say, "All that was committed to me, I am doing," just as Josiah did (v. 16).

Enable me to set my heart to seek You. Show me how to seek You through the Bible. Cleanse me, deal with my secret sin, pet sins, and wash me completely in truth. Your Word is life. Show me how I have neglected to obey it and failed to seek You through it. Teach me repentance, as You did Josiah. Let me be broken over my sin and let Your Word move me (v. 19).

Teach me what it means to worship You in spirit and in truth. Teach me humility and how to live humbly every day. Teach me how to maintain a tender heart toward You. Let Your Word become real to me and in me. Oh, Lord, send revival. Use Your Word to smash any idol. Break my heart with Your Word. Let tears flow freely from my eyes as I humble myself before You (vv. 26–27).

Father, may I daily interrupt my life to read Your Word (v. 30). Teach me to be obedient in whatever place of responsibility You have given me. Teach me to follow Your Word, and let me walk in covenant with You (v. 31). Use Your Word to bring strong conviction in me, and break me over my sin. Break me over the sin of my church. Use Your Word as a hammer to crush and to build up. Send revival, oh Lord, I pray (v. 33). In Jesus' name, amen.

Reflection Questions

1. Was there a time in your life when you rediscovered the Word of God that had been lost? Describe the period before and after your rediscovery.

2. What truth has God specifically shown you lately from the Bible?

3. After hearing God's Word preached, do you take time to medi-

tate and process it, or do you start talking about sports, weather, family, and so forth? What can you do to change that?

4. When was the last time you shared the Word of God with someone? What did you share?

5. Do you hold to the infallibility and inerrancy of Scripture but fail to live in the sufficiency of Scripture for your every need? What does the sufficiency of Scripture mean?

6. What practical changes do you need to make for Scripture to become sufficient for all your needs?

Chapter 11

REVIVAL under ZERUBBABEL: Experiencing Conviction

And when He is come, He will convict the world of sin, and of righteousness and of judgment: of sin, because they do not believe in Me; of righteousness, because I go to My Father and you see Me no more; of judgment, because the ruler of this world is judged. (John 16:8–11)

SCRIPTURE:
EZRA 1:1, 3, 5; 2:62; 3:1–2, 11

Now in the first year of Cyrus king of Persia, that the word of the Lord by the mouth of Jeremiah might be fulfilled, the Lord stirred up the spirit of Cyrus king of Persia, so that he made a proclamation throughout all his kingdom, and also *put it* in writing, saying . . . "Who *is* among you of all His people? May his God be with him, and let him go up to Jerusalem which *is* in Judah, and build the house of the Lord God of Israel (He *is* God), which *is* in Jerusalem."

Then the heads of the fathers' *houses* of Judah and Benjamin, and the priests and the Levites, with all whose spirits God had moved, arose to go up and build the house of the Lord which *is* in Jerusalem. . . .

These sought their listing *among* those who were registered by genealogy, but they were not found; therefore they *were excluded* from the priesthood as defiled. . . .

The people gathered as one man to Jerusalem. . . . arose and built the altar of the God of Israel, to offer burnt offerings on it, as *it is* written in the Law of Moses the man of God. . . .

And they sang responsively, praising and giving thanks to the LORD: "For *He is* good, For His mercy *endures* forever toward Israel." Then all the people shouted with a great shout, when they praised the LORD, because the foundation of the house of the LORD was laid.

Experiencing Conviction

David Hume, the eighteenth-century British philosopher who rejected historic Christianity, once met a friend hurrying along a London street and asked where he was going. The friend said he was off to hear George Whitfield preach. Hume said, "But surely you don't believe what Whitfield preaches do you?"

"No," his friend replied, "I don't, but he does."[21]

Conviction is crucial in revival. Apart from it, there is no revival. The first work of the Holy Spirit is conviction of sin. Pastor Michael Catt said, "Conviction that does not lead to confession is shallow. It may be remorse, but it is not repentance."[22]

The Bible tells us Jesus came to convict the world of sin, righteousness, and truth. Conviction of sin is that sense of dread in a life, not because of mere head knowledge that you have sinned, but a feeling of dreadfulness of what you have done to God. Though conviction makes us feel bad, thank God He convicts so we can see our sin. Without the convicting of the Holy Spirit, we are not even able to know our sin. Conviction is a powerful blessing. The Holy Spirit brings conviction often through the Word of God—by the Word being preached, taught, or quoted. Three things are common in all revivals: prayer, preaching, and the conviction of sin.

Because of Israel's sin, the nation went into captivity in Babylon for seventy years. The revival under Zerubbabel ushered in the return of the captives from Babylon and the beginning of the building of the second temple. When the people were set free from Babylonian captivity, only 7 percent, or about fifty thousand, chose to return to Jerusalem. Why? The Israelites had become accustomed to the things of their world, the world's influence and affluence. It was much easier to stay in Babylon than to travel some seven hundred miles back to Jerusalem. They chose to stay in their comfort zone.

One of the temptations we face today is of becoming too comfortable. We do not want to sacrifice to serve or obey God. We do not want to adjust our lives or lifestyle to the Word of God. We must realize, however, that if God is to be preeminent in all life, then everything is to flow around Him. Understanding God's will is crucial. When the conviction of God's Word comes to us, we will know what we are to do. We obey God's conviction by repenting of our sin and returning to God. We adjust our lives to Him, rather than trying to get Him to adjust to us.

Experiencing conviction of sin and conviction of truth are essential in knowing and walking with God, whether in speaker or listener. We know these only as we respond in obedience. The evidence of real revival is conviction that produces holiness in our lives.

Getting Personal

The first man to respond to God's conviction during the revival in Tennessee was Derek. He described his conviction experience this way:

One bullet. That would do it. My thought process had come down to this one expression. Over the last three to four years, I had degraded myself down to a point that I thought I was no longer worthy of life.

There was a time in my life that I was happy. I had a great wife, house, good job, close relationship with God and was pursuing a call to the ministry. Then I went through a divorce. My life honestly started imploding as I lost interest in everything. As I began to focus inward, I started distancing myself from my regular activities. My church sent ministry teams out to my house to talk with me and I was grateful to see them, but no matter what I just couldn't get the strength to return to church. Leaving the church was the first shovel of dirt out of the hole that I began to dig for myself to live in for the next three years.

I thought I was too broken to be of any use to others. I thought I was going to go insane. Anxiety attacks, lack of sleep, and the feeling of utter failure kept me anchored to a couch or bed. It was with great effort that I even went to work, and when I was there no one wanted to be around me because of my mood swings.

Where was God in all this? He was in the same place He had always been, in my heart. He would speak to me through people asking me to go back to church. When I would peek into church a few times over that period, He would always have a pleasant surprise waiting for me. One of my closest friends even wept when he asked me to return to God and the church, but I still managed to control the conviction. I knew Sunday where I needed to be and there weren't many days that went by when I wasn't convicted of needing to return to the family of God. I'm sure conviction was some of my misery, but God knows just how to love us back to Himself.

I was passing the church one day and noticed on the sign that there was a revival to be held soon. My whole plan was to ease back into church and after about one to two months of steady attendance, I would ask the church to forgive me for leaving, for I carried that burden as well.

I showed up the first night of the revival and the revivalist was preaching. So far, so good with my plan. I was so convicted over missing church and leaving God that during the sermon I went forward and confessed all my known sin; repented; and set my heart to stay in church from then on. Again, my plan was going well.

Once seated, the first words to hit my brain were *I can breathe again*. But that feeling stopped when Pastor Mark Partin asked me to come to the front. I didn't know what was going to happen, but I went up anyhow. I honestly can't really describe to you what happened next; I was in a fog. All I can remember was Partin getting down on his knees and touching my feet, saying, "Derek, please forgive us where we have failed you as the church, letting you go." When he touched my feet, it was like someone took a bucket of ice cold water and started from the top of my head and continued down to the bottom of my feet.

I sobbed and thought, *No, this isn't right, I left you!* but there was a voice inside my head that said "Accept this." I put my hands on Mark's shoulders, and he got up. I think I might have injured him when I hugged him so hard. Then, I asked the church to forgive me. I felt absolutely clean for the first time in a long time. So much for my plan. God had His own.

Additional Scripture on Experiencing Conviction

John 8:9; Titus 1:9; James 2:9; Jude 1:15

Scriptural Prayer for Revival

Merciful Savior, as in the days of Zerubbabel, so it is now. Your people are captive to the world and the world's system. It does not appear many want to respond to You or to follow You. Please move with strong conviction of sin, so we can see ourselves for what we truly are. Stir up our spirits. Raise up preachers to preach Your Word and let it burn in our hearts (Ezra 1:1).

Teach me Your sovereignty, please. You are in control, and You are working Your will for Your glory (v. 1). So let me always respond in obedience to Your Word and follow You wherever You lead (v. 3).

Father, let me seek less of my own kingdom and be a part of building Your kingdom. Give me understanding of what that means. Move on my spirit with Your Holy Spirit, so I also will be about Your business (v. 5).

Only You can send revival. But I ask, God, use me. Show me any sin that prevents me from being a useful vessel to You. Please, Father, do not exclude me because of my sin. Bring conviction of sin to my heart, and let me repent (2:62).

Father, teach us to come together as one, so we can build for Your kingdom and exalt Your glory. Teach me to bring an acceptable offering to You, Lord. Let me understand the importance of bringing a voluntary offering and sacrifice to You (3:1–2).

Give me an understanding of purpose, beyond my family and making a living. I want to be a vessel of praise, honor, and usefulness unto You (v. 11). Teach me to express myself, even with shouting aloud, for Your glory. Why is there so little shouting to Your glory in the church among Your people?

I thank You for Your provision, for Your grace and mercy. Again, I ask, move with conviction among Your people. Show Yourself mighty.

Be glorified. Father, send revival. In Jesus' name, amen.

Reflection Questions

1. Has God's Word ever been so real to you that it pointed its finger at you? How did you respond? How has your life changed since then?

2. If we ignore the convicting of the Holy Spirit, our hearts will become hard to the voice of God and the Word of God. What specific action must you take to maintain a receptive heart toward God and His Word?

3. Is there someone from whom you must ask forgiveness, or do you owe restitution to anyone? If so, describe the problem and what you will do to be obedient to God's conviction on you.

4. One of the devil's methods is to get us to compromise God's Word and ignore the Holy Spirit's conviction. What specific ways does the devil try to do this with you?

5. How does God's convicting affect your daily life? How does your life reflect your true convictions?

Chapter 12

REVIVAL under HAGGAI and ZECHARIAH: Preaching

I charge you therefore before God and the Lord Jesus Christ,
who will judge the living and the dead at His appearing
and His kingdom: Preach the word! Be ready in season. . . .
Convince, rebuke, exhort, with longsuffering and teaching.

(2 TIMOTHY 4:1–2)

SCRIPTURE:
HAGGAI 1:2–7; ZECHARIAH 1:1–6

"Thus speaks the LORD of hosts, saying: 'This people says, "The time has not come, the time that the LORD's house should be built."'"

Then the word of the LORD came by Haggai the prophet, saying, "*Is it* time for you yourselves to dwell in your paneled houses, and this temple *to lie* in ruins?" Now therefore, thus says the LORD of hosts: "Consider your ways! 'You have sown much, and bring in little; You eat, but do not have enough; You drink, but you are not filled with drink; You clothe yourselves, but no one is warm; And he who earns wages, Earns wages *to put* into a bag with holes.' Thus says the LORD of hosts: 'Consider your ways!'. . ."

In the eighth month of the second year of Darius, the word

of the Lord came to Zechariah the son of Berechiah, the son of Iddo the prophet, saying, "The Lord has been very angry with your fathers. Therefore say to them, 'Thus says the Lord of hosts: "Return to Me," says the Lord of hosts, "and I will return to you," says the Lord of hosts. "Do not be like your fathers, to whom the former prophets preached, saying, 'Thus says the Lord of hosts: "Turn now from your evil ways and your evil deeds."' But they did not hear nor heed Me," says the Lord.

"Your fathers, where *are* they? And the prophets, do they live forever? Yet surely My words and My statutes, Which I commanded My servants the prophets, Did they not overtake your fathers? So they returned and said: 'Just as the Lord of hosts determined to do to us, According to our ways and according to our deeds, So He has dealt with us.'"

Preaching Truth

Canadian pastor Oswald J. Smith said, "The world does not need sermons; it needs a message. You can go to seminary and learn how to preach a sermon, but you will have to go to God to get messages."[23]

Preaching is a calling from God to proclaim the truth of God's Word. It is both confrontational and comforting. It is foolishness to the world, but strong unto the glory of God. One can only preach with the anointing of the Holy Spirit as one is yielded to Christ and saturated in prayer, affecting both the message and the messenger.

We are not to preach pop psychology or human wisdom. We are to preach the infallible Word of God. Preaching is a means God uses in revival to confront people with His truth and draw them to Himself. The Bible promises the Word of God will not return void.

It will do what God intended for it to do, but not all listeners will respond as they should. David Wilkerson once had dinner with a fellow pastor. In the course of the conversation, this pastor confessed that he had not prayed for more than a year, yet he pastored 1,200 people. *Why,* Wilkerson wondered, *would anyone come to a church and listen to a man that does not pray?* And then he answered himself, saying, "You have 1,200 people not interested in being confronted with the truth of God's Word."[24]

What a terrible tragedy to experience the glory of God in revival, but then to stop, quit, fall short. Yet time and time again, we see that picture. Revival comes among the people of God, but at some point they get distracted with other things. They get caught up in building their own homes, and they forget God.

In our text, God's people had returned from Babylonian captivity to Jerusalem, laid the foundation and restored the altar, and offered sacrifices. God was sending revival among His people, but then they quit. They quit for fifteen years.

Boldly, with a prophet's voice, Haggai thundered: "Consider your ways!" (Haggai 1:5). God speaks to us through His Word as men preach and proclaim it boldly. Preaching confronts people with truth, God's truth. We are told in Romans 10:17, "Faith comes by hearing, and hearing by the word of God." But before that word is given, we find in Romans 10:15, "How shall they hear without a preacher?"

Preaching is a primary means God uses to move in a person and bring the person to understanding so that person can respond to God. Do you submit yourself to the preaching of the Word of God? Has God spoken to you and said, "Consider your ways"?

If you are experiencing a famine of satisfaction, consider your ways. Maybe you have a supportive and loving family, a good job, friends, but you just cannot seem to find any satisfaction in life. All you seem to know is a silent frustration. Are you dissatisfied most of the time? Maybe God is speaking to you, "Consider your ways." It is time we build God's kingdom and not our own. It is time to heed the preaching of God's Word.

Getting Personal

God calls men to preach. There is a difference between preaching and teaching. Sadly, many do not know the difference. Richard Owen Roberts told the following story in *Revival Commentary*:

> Over a period of some years, I was a frequent visitor in the home of a leading theological book seller in the United Kingdom whom I had taken to be a very placid man. Then one day he called me indicating he was going to visit the United States and would like to spend time with us in our home. We were delighted to be a part of his American itinerary. Upon my next visit to his home in England, I inquired concerning his impressions of this first visit to America. I was astonished at the vehemence of his response. In no uncertain terms he declared his great disappointment in not hearing a single preacher in America, albeit he had visited numerous churches in widely scattered areas. While he acknowledged hearing many teachers, he adamantly insisted he had not heard a single preacher. When I quietly asked, "What, in your opinion, is the difference between teaching and preaching?" I was amazed at the vigor with which he insisted, "It is not a matter of my opinion! It is a well-established fact! To teach is to inform! To preach is to move! I heard all kinds of teaching in America but I was never moved from where I am to where I ought to be!" Have you caught the distinction?[25]

To preach is to exhort. To exhort means to admonish with urgency. British itinerant preacher Arthur Wallis called this "apostolic preaching." He said apostolic preaching does not mean only the apostles preach that way. He said that kind of preaching was characteristic of first-century ministers and revivals throughout the years. Although souls are saved in revival apart from preaching, he said, revivals have always been characterized by powerful proclamations of God's truth.[26] Neither the Old Testament prophets nor New Testament apostles were popular, but both were mighty in pulling down Satan's strongholds.

We live in an age when many people want to replace the preached Word of God with other, more palatable things. God, however, has never promised to bless music, dramas, media, or Power Point presentations. God *has* promised that through the "foolishness of preaching" men can be saved. My words or my life do not have that promise, only the Word of God.

We are afraid of dogmatic preaching; yet, that is what we need. The Bible is dogmatic. The Word of God is dogmatic. When we go to a doctor for a medical problem, we want him or her to be dogmatic about the solution. We should want dogmatic preachers who stand and proclaim, "Thus says the Word of God." We need more than information. We need true biblical and "apostolic preaching" for there to be times of revival. We need preachers who will wield the Word of God with power and authority, and under the anointing of the Father. We are desperate for such preachers.

Additional Scripture on Preaching

Isaiah 61:1–2; Matthew 3:1–2, 4:17; Luke 9:2; Acts 8:12; Romans 16:25; 1 Corinthians 1:17–19

Scriptural Prayer for Revival

Compassionate Father, I so need to hear Your Word, and heed Your Word. Call out and raise up mighty and bold preachers of the gospel; as Haggai and Zechariah were Your preachers, we need bold preachers today. Show me any area where I have substituted my will for Your will. Teach me that the time is now to be about Your kingdom work (Haggai 1:2).

Please give unction to Your preachers, Your prophets. Let them proclaim Your Word with boldness and power, bringing glory to You (v. 3).

Father, do I allow Your temple to lie in ruins, in need of repair, while my home is pampered? Oh, Lord, let me consider my ways (v. 4).

Show me where I am investing my time and resources. Do I have true satisfaction, or do I get and get and yet still am not satisfied? Am I content with what I have? In what am I trying to find satisfaction? Food and drink? Money? Entertainment or sports? Things of the world (v. 6)?

Let me be careful to consider my ways before You. If my ways are not in complete alignment with Your ways, please forgive me. Show me where I need to change, and let me quickly adjust to You (v. 7).

Father, place strong preachers in my life, as Zechariah was in Israel's life (Zechariah 1:1).

Speak to me, Lord, and let me know my heart. Open my eyes, letting me see my true spiritual condition. Keep me sensitive to Your Word that I may live daily under repentance. Teach me Your sovereignty, for You are the Lord of hosts. Revive me through Your Word. Let me return to You at Your bidding (vv. 2–3).

Lord, do not let me excuse the way I live based on the way my parents lived. Let me not ignore Your words of warning or rebuke. May I

heed Your Word. Let me run to You and repent of my sin. Teach me
to hunger for Your preached Word. May Your prophets and preachers
be bold in proclamation (vv. 4–6). Deal with me according to my
ways. Father, send revival (v. 6). In Jesus' name, amen.

Reflection Questions

1. Hebrews 4:12 says, "The Word of God . . . is sharper than any
   two-edged sword." In what areas of your life has the preached
   Word of God confronted you?
2. In the church you attend, is sin strongly rebuked from the pulpit
   or is it seldom addressed? What specific sins are mentioned?
3. Does dogmatic preaching scare you? If so, why?
4. How can you recognize the difference between the preached
   Word of God and stories of man that merely tickle the ears?
   Explain the difference.
5. Do you pray earnestly for your preacher? What specific things
   do you pray for that person?

Chapter 13

REVIVAL under EZRA: Embracing Brokenness

The sacrifices of God are a broken spirit, A broken and a contrite heart—These, O God, You will not despise.

(PSALM 51:17)

SCRIPTURE:
EZRA 9:1–10

When these things were done, the leaders came to me, say-ing, "The people of Israel and the priests and the Levites have not separated themselves from the peoples of the lands, with respect to the abominations of the Canaanites, the Hittites, the Perizzites, the Jebusites, the Ammonites, the Moabites, the Egyptians, and the Amorites. For they have taken some of their daughters *as wives* for themselves and their sons, so that the holy seed is mixed with the peoples of *those* lands. Indeed, the hand of the leaders and rulers has been foremost in this tres-pass." So when I heard this thing, I tore my garment and my robe, and plucked out some of the hair of my head and beard, and sat down astonished. Then everyone who trembled at the words of the God of Israel assembled to me, because of the transgression of those who had been carried away captive, and I sat astonished until the evening sacrifice.

At the evening sacrifice I arose from my fasting; and having torn my garment and my robe, I fell on my knees and spread out my hands to the LORD my God. And I said: "O my God, I am too ashamed and humiliated to lift up my face to You, my God; for our iniquities have risen higher than *our* heads, and our guilt has grown up to the heavens. Since the days of our fathers to this day we *have been* very guilty, and for our iniquities we, our kings, *and* our priests have been delivered into the hand of the kings of the lands, to the sword, to captivity, to plunder, and to humiliation, as *it is* this day. And now for a little while grace has been *shown* from the LORD our God, to leave us a remnant to escape, and to give us a peg in His holy place, that our God may enlighten our eyes and give us a measure of revival in our bondage. For we *were* slaves. Yet our God did not forsake us in our bondage; but He extended mercy to us in the sight of the kings of Persia, to revive us, to repair the house of our God, to rebuild its ruins, and to give us a wall in Judah and Jerusalem. And now, O our God, what shall we say after this? For we have forsaken Your commandments."

Embracing Brokenness

Every person has an inborn determination to control his or her life. We want to be our own boss. But to experience revival, we must surrender to Christ, coming to Him on the terms that God's Word lays out for us. We yield our lives to Him. We learn to live the cross-style life; the crucified life. We learn to embrace the cross, embrace brokenness.

Roy Hession, a twentieth-century British preacher who embraced the need for repentance, said, "To be broken is the beginning of revival. It is painful, it is humiliating, but it is the only way."[27] Although brokenness is humiliating, God draws near to those who have a broken and contrite heart (Isaiah 57:15).

True brokenness is not a feeling or an emotion, although God does move on our emotions. Brokenness is not merely intellectual, but God does move on our intellect. Brokenness is not a sense of being wounded, although we may have been wounded. Brokenness is a constant awareness of our God-neediness. True brokenness requires a choice, an act of the will, as we respond to what God has done in our intellect and emotions. Brokenness is not a one-time choice, but an ongoing way of life. It is absolute surrender to the will of God. It is the stripping of all self: self-will, self-reliance, self-confidence, and selfishness. Only in brokenness can a person know and experience true revival. God allows us to go through intense seasons of brokenness to make us totally dependent on Christ. We will not meet God in revival until we meet Him in brokenness.

By the time of Ezra 9, God's people had already experienced great revival. The problem was they stopped. They backslid; they disobeyed the law of God. Ezra took the burden of his people's sins and came before God with honest confession. He was ashamed and humiliated. He was broken.

Why? Ezra had not committed these sins, but he was a vessel of the Lord. He had been captured by the Lord, so he became totally broken. Ezra 8:22–23 tells of his testimony to the king. After fasting, humbling himself, and seeking God, Ezra said, "The hand of God is upon all those who seek Him." To have God's hand on your life is to be captured by God, and then you surrender your will to His will.

Brokenness requires God's initiative and our response. God used three things to bring Ezra and Israel to brokenness. He used other believers (Ezra 9:1), and they named their sin. God used His revealed

Word (v. 4), and the people trembled at the Words of God. God used the circumstances of captivity and plunder (vv. 6–7). When Ezra explained the seriousness of their sin and their circumstances, the people responded to God.

When was the last time you responded publically to the Word of God? When was the last time you trembled at the Word of God? When was the last time you were embarrassed by church people's sin? When was the last time you were so captured by God that the sin of the church drove you to pray? When was the last time you heard honest, public confession of sin? When was the last time you confessed anything publically?

Getting Personal

During the Tennessee revival, Sandy came forward and the minister asked her what she needed. She told him she needed prayer for a physical condition. As he talked with her, he said, "You have a judgmental and critical spirit."

I was standing next to him when he said that, and my eyes widened with surprise. I waited to see her response. She seemed unfazed. The three of us prayed, and she returned to her seat. Little did I know how God used those few words to initiate brokenness in her life. This is what she said:

> I left the church that night, more miserable than ever. I actually became angry and offended as I thought about what had been said. My critical spirit was certainly a reality now. The Holy Spirit was revealing my pride and selfishness finally to me. I prayed all night. I began to see myself though God's eyes. I could see how badly I was breaking my Savior's heart and delaying fulfillment of His will for my life. I began to cry and purge all self-centered

idolatry. The view of myself through God's eyes literally made me vomit. I was finally free. Finally, I could see what God was doing in my life. God had to initiate brokenness in my life and I had to yield to Him in order for Him to prepare me for future service.

Brokenness gave me an entirely new perspective. I had a new perspective about God, my loving heavenly Father, and I had a new perspective for my life. Before brokenness, I had an attitude of self-reliance, self-righteousness, and self-centeredness. I was miserable on the inside, but to the world I appeared successful in every way. Pride was definitely a stronghold on my life. It was only as I asked others to pray for me that I was able to totally surrender that area of my life to God. Yet that area controlled all the other areas. Hallelujah I am free![28]

The greatest hindrance to revival is not other people who refuse to humble themselves, but our refusal to humble ourselves and confess our need to God. You will not meet God in revival until you meet Him in brokenness.

Additional Scripture on Brokenness
Isaiah 57:15; John 12:24–25; Philippians 2:3–4; James 4:8–10

Scriptural Prayer for Revival
Oh Lord, Your people need revival; revive us again. Father, show me what it means to separate myself from the world and its ways. Teach me true surrender to You (Ezra9:1).

Show me the last time I was moved to astonishment over sin, my sin, and over my church's sin. Teach me, Lord, how to give You control of my life, my time, my thoughts, my finances, my money, my family. Lord, tomorrow teach me to do it again, afresh. May I be broken; let remorse and sorrow be evident in my life, just as it was in Ezra's life (v. 3).

Father, let me tremble at Your Word. Let conviction flow forth (v. 4). Capture me for Your glory, just as You did with Ezra. Let me know purity—purity of speech, thoughts, and lifestyle. Let me take every thought captive unto Your glory. Teach me to fall on my knees before You, and to raise my hands in honor and out of my emptiness before You. Oh, Lord, I need You (vv. 5–6).

Show me my sin. Burden me over it. Let brokenness manifest itself in me. Break down the strongholds of pride, greed, and lust. Wash me, Lord. Let me see my own humiliation (v. 6).

Burden me for the condition of the church, Your bride. Oh, Lord, she is to be without spot or blemish. Purify Your church; send revival to Your church. Father, enlighten my eyes so I can know Your way and have discernment, so Your church can see (v. 8).

Oh God, give us revival at any cost. Do not forsake us in our bondage. I surrender to You. Break me unto Your glory. Revive me, and extend mercy to me. As we rebuild out of the ruins, give us a wall of strong understanding, a wall of doctrinal purity, a wall of refuge (v. 9). Revive us, Lord. In Jesus' name, amen.

Reflection Questions

1. What evidence is there in your life that your will, mind, emotions, and actions are controlled by God?

2. What are you withholding from God? Money? Children? Marriage? Time? What must you do to change this?

3. What activities or pastime do you justify because your children enjoy it, yet it takes you away from the church? What habits,

REVIVAL UNDER EZRA   **107**

attitudes, or beliefs do you rationalize that are contrary to the Word of God?

4. When was the last time you were so humbled and broken that you could not lift your head before the Lord?

5. Every day we must embrace brokenness. Do you? How is brokenness in you evidenced at your workplace? With your family?

Chapter 14

REVIVAL under NEHEMIAH: Living in Unity

That they all may be one, as You, Father, are in Me, and I
in You; that they may also be one in Us, that the world may
believe that You sent Me. And the glory which You gave Me
I have given them, that they may be one just as We are one.

(JOHN 17:21–22)

SCRIPTURE:
NEHEMIAH 1:3–11; 8:1, 6–8; 9:1–3

And they said to me [Nehemiah], "The survivors who are left from the captivity in the province *are* there in great distress and reproach. The wall of Jerusalem *is* also broken down, and its gates are burned with fire."

So it was, when I heard these words, that I sat down and wept, and mourned *for many* days; I was fasting and praying before the God of heaven.

And I said: "I pray, LORD God of heaven, O great and awesome God, *You* who keep *Your* covenant and mercy with those who love You and observe Your commandments, please let Your ear be attentive and Your eyes open, that you may hear the prayer of Your servant which I pray before You now, day and night, for the children of Israel Your servants, and confess the sins of the children of Israel which we have sinned against You. Both my father's house and I have sinned. We have acted very corruptly against You, and have not kept the commandments, the statutes, nor the ordinances which You commanded Your servant Moses. Remember, I pray, the word that You commanded Your servant Moses, saying, 'If you are unfaithful, I will scatter you among the nations; 'but if you return to Me, and keep My commandments and do them, though some of you were cast out to the farthest part of the heavens, yet I will gather them from there, and bring them to the place which I have chosen as a dwelling for My name.' Now these are Your servants and Your people, whom You have redeemed by Your great power, and by Your strong hand. O Lord, I pray, please let Your ear be attentive to the prayer of Your servant, and to the prayer of Your servants who desire to fear Your name; and let Your servant prosper this day, I pray, and grant him mercy in the sight of this man."

For I was the king's cupbearer.

Now all the people gathered together as one man in the open square that was in front of the Water Gate; and they told Ezra the scribe to bring the Book of the Law of Moses, which the LORD had commanded to Israel.

And Ezra blessed the LORD, the great God.

Then all the people answered, "Amen, Amen!" while lifting up their hands. And they bowed their heads and worshiped the LORD with their faces to the ground.

Also Jeshua, Bani, Sherebiah, Jamin, Akkub, Shabbethai, Hodijah, Maaseiah, Kelita, Azariah, Jozabad, Hanan, Pelaiah, and the Levites, helped the people to understand the Law; and the people stood in their place. So they read distinctly from the book, in the Law of God; and they gave the sense, and helped *them* to understand the reading.

Now on the twenty-fourth day of this month the children of Israel were assembled fasting, in sackcloth, and with dust on their heads. Then those of Israelite lineage separated themselves from all foreigners; and they stood and confessed their sins and the iniquities of their fathers. And they stood up in their place and read from the Book of the Law of the LORD their God *for one*-fourth of the day; and *for another* fourth they confessed and worshiped the LORD their God.

Living and Performing in Unity

The human body functions in harmony when it is healthy, with every organ doing what it is purposed to do. Similarly, the unity that the Bible speaks of flows from the body of Christ, as every member is under the headship of Christ Jesus. When each member of the body (the church) is under the control of the head, we function together as one. Headship and lordship go together. You cannot have one without the other. As the world sees the unity of the body of Christ, they will know Christ is God and be drawn to Him (John 17:23).

Acts 2:1 says, "When the day of Pentecost was fully come, they [the disciples] were all with one accord in one place." In the Greek, "one accord" means symphony. A symphony is when all instruments perform together in harmony around a single theme. For believers, that theme is the glory of God. Each believer performs according to his or her gifting and characteristics, yet we all play together in harmony, guided by our conductor, the Holy Spirit. The result of this harmony is unity.

God used Nehemiah to accomplish a daunting and seemingly impossible task. He returned with the people of God from exile with the burden of God to rebuild the walls of Jerusalem. These walls had lain in ruins ninety years. Without these walls, the people were defenseless and vulnerable to any threat. They also lacked any line of demarcation or separation from the world.

Rebuilding the wall took fifty-two days as God's man followed God's direction and gave leadership to the people. But Nehemiah did not stop there. Sensitive to God's direction, he gave center stage to Ezra the scribe (Nehemiah 8:1) so he could preach: "Now all the people gathered together as one man in the open square that *was* in front of the Water Gate." The phrase "as one man" means they had unity.

Humans cannot produce unity; only God can produce it. Unity is a result of God's people seeking intimacy with Christ. When we lose our intimacy with God, there will be a loss of unity among believers. When God's people are willing to live in one accord, revival can be realized. In our focal passage, God's remnant people had responded to Him. They had returned from captivity. They had rebuilt the temple. Now the walls of Jerusalem, the Holy City, were completed. Nehemiah led the physical revival by rebuilding the wall, while Ezra led the spiritual revival of the nation.

When Ezra began to preach in chapter 9, the people were hungry for the Word of God. He preached for six hours as they stood. The next day they did it again for three hours. This went on for a month. Ezra and others preached and taught the Word of God for three hours; and then the people confessed their sin, repented, and worshipped God for three hours. This constant exposure to the Word of God brought revival as they responded to the proclaimed Word. Revival comes when you say, "Lord, I surrender all I am to You. I am not much, but I am Yours. Use me for Your glory. I give myself to You."

Getting Personal

I have been pastor at my present church for twenty years. My family and I came to this church in January 1993. When we arrived, it was struggling. We knew it was a hard situation, but we also knew God had specifically called us here.

During the last pastor's tenure, little groups had emerged. Each group thought they knew best for the church. After that pastor left, there was an interim of about eighteen months before we arrived. At first, everyone was so gracious, loving, and encouraging. They seemed to want the church to turn around and prosper in the Lord. They were desperate for God to move.

Then, after we had been here for a few months, we could see the groups. No one told us about them, but we noticed. The scene was similar to what I imagine Mordecia Ham, an American evangelist, was describing when he said: "One of our troubles is we are not willing to humble ourselves. We are not willing to give up our opinions as to how things should be done. We want a revival to come just in our way. You never saw two revivals come just alike. We must let them come in God's way."[29]

Today, those groups are nonthreatening and vanishing. They have relinquished their hold. How did this happen? Several things took place. First, God let the people get to a point of desperation for Him. One man told me, "Preacher, we cannot afford another mistake." They were also hungry for someone to lead them and be their shepherd. Desperation does things like that. Therefore, my concentration was, and still is, to feed the flock with the Word of God. God may have pastors do many things, but preaching the Word must be foremost.

Just as it was in Nehemiah and Ezra's day, so it is today. The constant exposure to the Word of God ignites a hunger for God. When we are hungry for God, we seek intimacy with God. A oneness of mind and heart develops and unity is the by-product. I began to disciple the people, using tools such as *Experiencing God* and *Master Life* (Bible-based discipleship studies). The discipleship groups multiplied. Finally, after several years, more than one hundred adults have gone through the *Experiencing God* study. As a result, people began to understand the purpose of the church and everyone seemed to get on the same page, so to speak. Personal preference was no longer as important as God and God's kingdom purpose. Oneness of purpose and unity is emerging.

In revival, unity is a natural expression that flows from the people of God.

Additional Scripture on Unity

Psalm 133:1; Ecclesiastes 4:9–10; John 17:21–22; 1 Corinthians 1:10; Ephesians 4:3, 13

Scriptural Prayer for Revival

Gracious Father, give me eyes to see the true condition of Your people. Help me to see myself and my family as You do. Does my heart breaks over the things of this world, or am I broken over the spiritual condition of Your people? Am I more burdened over personal needs than for Your kingdom and Your glory? (Nehemiah 1:3–4).

Father, just as Nehemiah was overwhelmed by the needs of his people, overwhelm me. Stop me in my tracks, and let me see what characterizes my life and the lives of Your people. Teach me to fast and pray, to intercede for the church (v. 4).

You are a great and awesome God. You are the eternal and

omnipotent God, and I bless Your name. Oh, Lord, intervene in Your church. Send revival and move among us. Let me understand that You keep covenant and are merciful to those who love You. If we love You, we will obey You (v. 5).

Teach me the necessity of prayer. Teach me the necessity of confession of sin, both personal and corporate sin. Let me understand how sin among the body of Christ affects us and hinders us. Let me see how ruthlessly sin corrupts (vv. 6–7).

Father, teach me how to plead Your Word, Your promises in prayer (v. 8).

Let the church return to You with biblical repentance (v. 9).

Oh Lord, constantly remind me how You redeemed me by Your power. Let me be faithful to praise You for Your mighty acts (v. 10).

Prosper me in faith and spiritual understanding. Teach me Your Word. Give me fresh understanding and insight. Show me that I can be an instrument of revival, just like Nehemiah, a cupbearer, a common man (v. 11).

Show me how to submit to the leadership You place in the church. Keep me teachable. I long to know You and to grow in intimacy with You. Let Your church have that same hunger for You, so unity will flow forth as a result. Let our unity be a strong testimony to the world of Your wisdom, Your greatness and glory (8:1).

Oh, Lord, let me be attentive to Your Word. May it be fresh to my spirit. Teach me not to be ashamed to lift my hands to praise Your name; I worship You, my God. I give You honor and praise. I bless Your name. Father, give me assurance that You hear my prayers, and that You are attentive to them (v. 6).

Let me not grow weary in praying. If I do, prompt me quickly by Your Holy Spirit. And show me how to confess corporate sin to You

(v. 7). Unite Your church as we worship You. Teach us and give us understanding of Your Word, as we stand in our place, in our position of responsibility. Lord, I testify Your Word is absolute truth (vv. 7–8).

Father, teach me to respond to Your Word with repentance. Teach me the importance of fasting, making You my priority. Enable me to understand brokenness over my sin (9:1).

Show me anyone or anything from which I am to separate myself; anything that causes me to compromise my walk with You (v. 2).

Oh, Lord, give me a daily hunger for Your Word, and show me how to respond to Your Word with confession of sin and worship (v. 3). In Jesus' name, amen.

Reflection Questions

1. When was the last time you wept or mourned over the condition of the church in America? Over your local church?
2. Does your local church display unity? If not, why not? If so, how?
3. We are commanded in Scripture to endeavor "to keep the unity of the Spirit in the bond of peace" (Ephesians 4:3). How can you do this?
4. How do you respond to discord in the church?
5. The constant exposure to the Word of God, be it preached, taught, or read and digested, keeps us hungering after the Lord and brings unity among the brethren. How do you keep yourself exposed to Scripture so this will be true of you?
6. What is God saying to you today?

Chapter 15

REVIVAL under JOHN the BAPTIST: Repenting

*Now I rejoice, not that you were made sorry, but that your
sorrow led to repentance. For you were made sorry in a godly
manner, that you might suffer loss from us in nothing. For
godly sorrow produces repentance leading to salvation, not
to be regretted; but the sorrow of the world produces death.*

(2 CORINTHIANS 7:9–10)

SCRIPTURE:
MATTHEW 3:1–3, 7–11

In those days John the Baptist came preaching in the wilderness
of Judea, and saying, "Repent, for the kingdom of heaven is at
hand!" For this is he who was spoken of by the prophet Isaiah,
saying: "The voice of one crying in the wilderness: 'Prepare the
way of the LORD; Make His paths straight.'"

But when he saw many of the Pharisees and Sadducees
coming to his baptism, he said to them, "Brood of vipers! Who
warned you to flee from the wrath to come? Therefore bear fruits
worthy of repentance, and do not think to say to yourselves, 'We
have Abraham as *our* father.' For I say to you that God is able to
raise up children to Abraham from these stones. And even now
the ax is laid to the root of the trees. Therefore every tree which

does not bear good fruit is cut down and thrown into the fire. I indeed baptize you with water unto repentance, but He who is coming after me is mightier than I, whose sandals I am not worthy to carry. He will baptize you with the Holy Spirit and fire.

Repenting and Changing

Repentance is a military term from the Romans that means to turn around. Thus, as the grace of God is extended toward us, we are to turn from our sin, self, and the world to Jesus Christ by faith. Repentance is an indispensable principle in revival.

In his book *I Surrender*, Patrick Morley wrote that the church's integrity problem is in the misconception "that we can add Christ to our lives, but not subtract sin. It is a change in belief without a change in behavior." He goes on to say, "It is revival without reformation, without repentance."[30]

Repentance is the first word of the gospel. John the Baptist came preaching repentance, and it is the last word Jesus Christ gave to the church in Revelation 2. Repentance is the way a lost person comes to Christ for salvation, and it is the way a saved person lives daily.

Repentance involves our total being: mind, will, and emotions. The Bible tells us that godly sorrow produces repentance (2 Corinthians 7:10). In contrast, the sorrow of the world produces death. Even though the process of repenting may make us feel miserable, never forget repentance is a gift of God and we should thank Him for it. Without biblical repentance, we cannot know God nor can we be right with God. Revival never occurs without repentance.

When I study Scripture, I am amazed by the number of men who had wilderness experiences. Joseph found himself in a wilderness of Egyptian slavery and prison. Moses was literally in a wilderness forty years, on the backside of the desert. Elijah went to the brook of Cherith for three years. David was anointed king and went back to the wilderness with his sheep. John the Baptist came from the wilderness. Jesus was led by the Holy Spirit into the wilderness. Paul, after his conversion, went to the wilderness (desert) of Arabia for several years before returning to seek out the disciples.

Everyone God uses greatly has to go through their own wilderness, the wilderness of preparation. In the wilderness, we learn our spiritual weapons: the Word of God and praying in faith. We learn dependency on the Father. We learn what it means to be separated to God. We also learn humility (Deuteronomy 8:2). The wilderness gives birth to real men and women of God.

You will not have to look for your wilderness when you surrender completely to God. He will get you there. What you have to do is be willing to stay there until your lessons are learned. Wilderness experiences can come more than once in a lifetime. Have you been in a wilderness lately? If so, take heart.

When John came, he preached repentance from sin and dead works. Sin we understand, but what are dead works? Dead works are anything we think helps in our salvation or enables us to maintain our salvation. Our salvation is secure in Christ and not maintained by our works. The New Testament speaks of works of the flesh (Galatians 5:19), as well as dead works (Hebrews 6:1). Both these types of works are deceitful. They can be good things we are doing, but they spring from a corrupt motive or we do them for the wrong reasons. We are commanded not only to repent of sin but also from dead works (Hebrews 9:14).

John the Baptist told us that we are to "bear fruits worthy of repentance" (Matthew 3:8). What does that mean? Let me suggest five deeds or attitudes appropriate as fruits worthy of repentance:

- An absence of rationalization for sin. We stop making excuses (1 John 1:6, 10).
- A *genuine* sorrow over our sins (2 Corinthians 7:9).
- The open confession of sin. Sinners who are repentant want to make things right with those they have hurt. There is no attempt to hide the sin (1 John 1:9).
- Restitution, or at least an attempt at restitution, is made. (2 Corinthians 2:11).
- A hatred of our sin. Hatred to the point we avoid it at all cost (2 Timothy 2:2).

Getting Personal

Several years ago, a revivalist and I went to visit Clifford. Clifford was an unsaved man in his seventies. I had tried unsuccessfully to talk to Clifford in the past about his spiritual state. Today proved to be no different than my past visits. He was blunt, saying, "I'm not interested in anything you have to say." Then he shut the door in our faces.

I continued praying for Clifford and even attempted to talk to him again to no avail. One day, I received a phone call from a fellow pastor who said, "I'm visiting Clifford, and he said he wanted to talk to you."

"Why?" I replied. "I don't even think he likes me." But I made the trip to Clifford's home one more time. He needed some hospital test, because doctors thought he might have cancer. Although he was concerned, he was not interested in being saved. I prayed for him. As I left I thought, *That's my last time going to see Clifford.*

A few weeks later, I received another call, and Clifford wanted to see me again. I went back to his home. All the tests had been run, and he and his family, many of whom were believers, were waiting for the results. His diagnosis did not look good. Clifford said he was willing to listen if I explained the way of salvation as long as no one else was in the room. So I asked his family to step outside.

I will never forget sitting at his kitchen table reading Scripture, explaining salvation, and praying silently nonstop for wisdom. We talked about sin and the conviction of the Holy Spirit. We talked about repentance. We talked about forgiveness.

At last, Clifford said, "I want to be saved." He prayed his own prayer of faith. I will never forget how he started his prayer. He bowed his head and clasped his hands together under his chin, and said, "God, this is Clifford ———. I need you to save me. . . ." He confessed his sin and called out to God for forgiveness. At the news, his family praised God with tears of joy.

Was I certain Clifford was saved? No. I knew his health was bad. I prayed that he had responded to God's grace with true faith. Soon, I would see the fruit of biblical repentance, real change.

That week, Clifford was diagnosed with cancer. Sunday morning he was in church, smiling from ear to ear. I had never seen him smile. He always had been stone-faced and distant, but he came to the front of the church and gave me a big hug. Then, I saw him going around talking to everyone and hugging them. Clifford was beginning to show fruit of his newfound faith in Jesus Christ. That week, he went into his bank and his pharmacy and apologized to the workers for how rude he had been to them over the years.

As I talked to his family at his funeral, I told them, "Before he was saved, I don't think he liked me."

"He didn't like anyone before he got saved," they replied. What a change came to his life upon salvation. That is what repentance and faith in Christ does; it brings change.

Repentance is the first message of the gospel, delivered by John the Baptist. Repentance is also the last admonition Jesus gave to the church in Revelation 2. Repentance is crucial to God's church for knowing and continuing in revival.

Additional Scripture on Repenting

Luke 5:32; Acts 5:31; 1 Peter 2:25; Revelation 2:5

Scriptural Prayer for Revival

Lord of Glory, I thank You for the preached word. Let me understand how it calls me to repentance. Give me a fresh hunger for Your preached word. Oh God, we need revival. I need revival. Show me how to repent and come before You. Repentance is a gift, and without it, I can never be right with You. Thank You for repentance although it appears so unpleasant (Matthew 3:1–2).

Father, teach me how to prepare Your way and make Your paths straight. Since preparing Your way begins with my heart, Lord, let me prepare. Let me understand how time is short and how close is the kingdom of heaven (v. 3).

Thank You for confronting and convicting me with truth. Continue to transform me by Your Word. Show me how to adjust my life and lifestyle to You. Let me know fruit worthy of repentance and see evidence of it in my life (vv. 7–8). Let me be earnest for You and indignant about sin. Lord, give me a consuming longing for You. Teach me restitution, and let me not avenge my wrongs. (2 Corinthians 7:11).

Oh, Lord, may I bear good fruit. May Your axe fall and consume anything in me that is not of You (Matthew 3:10).

Father, let me not get so comfortable with You that I think I am worthy to carry Your sandals. Pour out Your Spirit on my life. Wash me, forgive me, cleanse me, and use me. Wherever You lead me, I will follow. May I bear good fruit for Your glory. Prune me. Baptize me with Your Holy Spirit, completely immersing me in You. Baptize me with fire. Cleanse me, purify me, and make me completely Yours (v. 11). Be glorified through my life. Send a revival of repentance to Your church. In Jesus' name, amen.

Reflection Questions

1. Explain how biblical repentance involves your emotions, will, and intellect.
2. What is the last thing you repented of?
3. If you fail to practice genuine biblical repentance, Christ will never be Lord of your life. What evidence is there in your life that would indicate that Jesus Christ is your Lord?
4. Esau did not find an opportunity for repentance afterward even "though he sought it diligently with tears" (Hebrews 12:17). Why can time run out to repent of our sins?
5. What dead works are demonstrated in your life? What will you do about that?

Chapter 16

REVIVAL under PETER at PENTECOST: Filling by the Holy Spirit

And I will pray the Father, and He will give you another Helper, that He may abide with you forever—the Spirit of truth, whom the world cannot receive, because it neither sees Him nor knows Him; but you know Him, for He dwells with you and will be in you. I will not leave you orphans; I will come to you. (JOHN 14:16–18)

SCRIPTURE:
ACTS 2:1–4

When the Day of Pentecost had fully come, they were all with one accord in one place. And suddenly there came a sound from heaven, as of a rushing mighty wind, and it filled the whole house where they were sitting. Then there appeared to them divided tongues, as of fire, and *one* sat upon each of them. And they were all filled with the Holy Spirit and began to speak with other tongues, as the Spirit gave them utterance.

Being Filled with the Holy Spirit

Several years ago, a member of a church I pastored told me he was afraid of the Holy Spirit. That struck me as strange because he was an ordained minister and a leader in state denominational work. Yet he said he "was afraid of the Holy Spirit" because of the excesses he had observed by others who claimed to be filled with the Holy Spirit.

The Holy Spirit is not a force or an influence or a power. The Holy Spirit is a person. You never have to be afraid of the Holy Spirit. He will always lead you the right way, in what is best for you and for the kingdom of God. His leading may not always be at a convenient time nor may it always be pleasant, but it will always be right and God's will.

In Ephesians 5:18, we are commanded to "be filled with the Spirit." Since this is a command, it also means it is possible not to be filled, which means we can lose the fullness of the Holy Spirit. In the Greek, the word "filled" is present tense, and therefore means an ongoing action. So we are daily commanded to be filled with the Holy Spirit.

D. L Moody said, "I believe firmly that the moment our hearts are emptied of pride and selfishness and ambition and everything that is contrary to God's law, the Holy Spirit will fill every corner of our hearts. But if we are full of pride and conceit and ambition and the world, there is no room for the Spirit of God. We must be emptied before we can be filled."[31]

In John 20:22, Jesus breathed on the disciples and they received the Holy Spirit. Later, according to Acts 1:8, Christ told them they would receive power after the Holy Spirit came upon them. This power shows that something is happening on the inside (power) that brings results on the outside (they would be witnesses of Christ).

How are we filled with the Holy Spirit? In Acts 2, the disciples were already Christians, and they knew it. Lost people, sinners, are not filled with the Spirit. To be filled with the Holy Spirit, we must know we are truly saved. Next, we have to be convicted of our need to be filled.

Filling Daily

If you think you can live the Christian life by being moral and by keeping a set of rules, you are mistaken. The disciples waited for ten days, hiding in fear in Jerusalem. They were afraid because this was the very city that crucified Christ; they waited in a hostile place, but they waited in obedience. The disciples were desperate; they knew they needed more of God, not only with them but in them. If you are satisfied with where you are, you probably will not know the filling and fullness of the Holy Spirit. If you say "I will do this" or "I will not do that," you cannot be filled with the Holy Spirit. When you say "I will or "I will not," you are in control. Being filled with the fullness of the Holy Spirit depends on being a yielded vessel. When you are a yielded vessel, you give up control and respond in obedience and submission to God. You have an attitude of surrender and humility.

The next step is repentance. Repentance is a change of heart, mind, and attitude. It is an act of your will where you willingly surrender all to the lordship of Jesus Christ. You stop going through the motions and surrender everything to Christ Jesus, giving God complete control of your life. Luke 11:13 says, "How much more will *your* heavenly Father give the Holy Spirit to those who ask Him!" To be filled with the Holy Spirit, you simply ask. This means you want Him. If you do not ask, He will not come.

Finally, you must believe that you are filled. As you are obedient to the Word of God and you live daily under repentance, God fills you with the Holy Spirit. It is the will of God for you to be filled with the Holy Spirit. You do not have to feel it or see it, but you can know you are if you are daily surrendering 100 percent to Christ. You know the Spirit's filling by faith as you live in obedience to the Word of God.

God sends the Holy Spirit to enable us to live the Christian life and glorify Christ. The results of being filled with the Holy Spirit are power, boldness, and a new awareness and sensitivity to the things of God. Christ becomes your life (Colossians 3:1) and the fruit of the Holy Spirit is evidenced in your life (Galatians 5:22–23). Also, you know complete rest (Hebrews 3:18–4:2): rest of heart, rest of mind, and rest of body.

We all need the filling of the Holy Spirit daily. We must appropriate this filling by faith and seek the experience. If the filling tarries, we must continue to persevere in faith, believing God has given us the fullness and He will also release this blessing in experience.

Grieving the Spirit

We can grieve the Holy Spirit, quench the Holy Spirit, resist the Holy Spirit, and even blaspheme the Holy Spirit. All of these are accomplished by sin working in a person's life when we fail to deal with our sin, leaving it unconfessed and unforsaken. In Ezekiel 36:25–26, God promised that He will cleanse us. Then, after this cleansing, He will put His Spirit within us, or He will fill us with His Holy Spirit. In verse 27, we are told why we are cleansed and then filled: The Lord says, "I will . . . cause you to walk in My statues, and you will keep My judgments and do *them*."

The fullness of the Holy Spirit must be sought, received, and kept so that we can be saturated and filled with God. This saturation and filling of the Holy Spirit enables us to know and do the will of God.

Only when we are cleansed and then filled can God enable us to do His work.

Getting Personal

In *The Life of D. L. Moody*, there is a simple but striking account of D. L. Moody's secret enduement of power. Oh, how he was filled with the Holy Spirit:

The year 1871 was a critical one in Mr. Moody's career. He realized more and more how little he was fitted by personal acquirements for his work. An intense hunger and thirst for spiritual power were aroused in him by two women who used to attend the meetings and sit on the front seat. He could see by the expression on their faces that they were praying. At the close of the services they would say to him:

"We have been praying for you." "Why don't you pray for the people?" Moody would ask. "Because you need the power of the Spirit," they would say. "I need the power! Why," said Mr. Moody, in relating the incident years after, "I thought I had the power. I had the largest congregation in Chicago, and there were many conversions. I was in a sense satisfied. But right along those two godly women kept praying for me, and their earnest talk about anointing for special service set me to thinking. I asked them to come and talk with me, and they poured out their hearts in prayer that I might receive the filling of the Holy Spirit. There came a great hunger into my soul. I did not know what it was. I began to cry out as I never did before. I really felt that I did not want to live if I could not have this power for service."

The hunger for spiritual power was upon Moody. "My heart was not into begging," Moody said. "I could not appeal. I was crying all the time that God would fill me with His Spirit. Well, one day, in the city of New York—oh, what a day!—I cannot describe it, I seldom refer to it; it is almost too sacred an experience to name. Paul had an experience which he never spoke of for fourteen years. I can only say that God revealed Himself to me, and I had such an experience of love that I had to ask Him to stay His hand. I went to preaching again. The sermons were not different; I did not present any new truths, yet hundreds were converted. I would not now be placed back where I was before that blessed experience if you give me all the world—it would be as the dust of the balance."[32]

If D. L. Moody needed the filling of the Holy Spirit, how much more should we seek it?

Evan Roberts, the coal miner God raised up mightily to begin the Welsh Revival of the early 1900s, was filled with the Holy Spirit. "For thirteen years," writes Evan Roberts, "I prayed for the Spirit; and this is the way I was led to pray. William Davies, the deacon, said one night in the society: 'Remember to be faithful. What if the Spirit descended and you were absent? Remember Thomas! What a loss he had!'

"I said to myself: 'I will have the Spirit' and through every kind of weather and in spite of all difficulties, I went to the meetings. Many times, on seeing other boys with the boats on the tide, I was tempted to turn back and join them. But, no. I said to myself: 'Remember your resolve,' and on I went. I went faithfully to the meetings for prayer throughout the ten or eleven years I prayed for Revival. It was the Spirit that moved me thus to think."

At a certain morning meeting that Evan Roberts attended,

the evangelist, in one of his petitions, besought that the Lord would "bend" them. The Spirit seemed to say to Roberts: "That's what you need, to be bent." Roberts says he "felt a living force coming into my bosom. This grew and grew, and I was almost bursting. My bosom was boiling. What boiled in me was the verse: 'God commending His love.' I fell on my knees with my arms over the seat in front of me; the tears and perspiration flowed freely. I thought blood was gushing forth."

Certain friends approached to wipe his face.

Meanwhile he cried out, "O Lord, bend me! Bend me!" Then suddenly the glory broke. Roberts adds, "After I was bent, a wave of peace came over me, and the audience sang, 'I hear Thy welcome voice.' And as they sang I thought about the bending at the Judgment Day, and I was filled with compassion for those that would have to bend on that day, and I wept. Henceforth, the salvation of souls became a burden of my heart. From that time I was on fire with a desire to go through all Wales."[33]

The experience of these two men shows us the need to be filled with the Holy Spirit. We need His filling, so we can experience the enduement from God and serve Him with effectiveness. The key is to seek God and ask God for filling. For these men, their filling was a decisive moment after having sought and asked God for His fullness.

This is how F. B. Meyer, a frequent preacher at the Keswick Convention in the late 1800s, experienced the filling of the Holy Spirit. In November 1884, speaking in reference to C. T. Studd and Stanley Smith of the Cambridge Seven, at thirty-seven years of age and a seasoned pastor, Meyers said:[34]

I saw that these young men had something that I did not, but which was to them a constant source of rest and peace. So I asked them, "How can I be like you?" Charley Studd inquired if Meyer had ever "given yourself to Christ, for Christ to fill you?" Meyer replied, "Yes, in a general sort of way, but I don't know what I have done particularly."

One evening after the close of the official meeting a number of us remained for prayer in the Tent and, because Grubb led them, grew vociferous. Meyer crept "under the tent" and walked into the night—up Manor Brow and towards the higher ground—feeling "the time had come when I must have everything or have a broken heart. . . . I walked to and fro, and said to God: 'I must have the best, I cannot go on living like this.' He seemed to hear God's voice to his soul, 'Breath in the air, breath it in; and as you breath it in your lungs, let there be an intake from God.'" . . . In the quiet of the hillside he opened his whole being to God.

He felt no surge of feeling. "Though I do not feel it," he said, "I reckon God is faithful," and his ministry from thenceforth showed him right.

I believe many Christians have given themselves to Christ in a "general sort of way." We must get specific about the Holy Spirit filling our lives daily, moment by moment. As the hymn writer said, "All is vain unless the Spirit of the Holy comes down." We must be filled with the Holy Spirit. We must continually seek His fullness.

Additional Scripture on Being Filled with the Holy Spirit

John 14:26, 15:26–27, 16:5–14; Acts 1:1–8; 2 Corinthians 13:14; Colossians 3:15–16

Scriptural Prayer for Revival

God of Grace, I need Your presence and fullness in my life. Fill me afresh with Your Holy Spirit. Let revival begin in me. Father, the church needs an outpouring of Your presence, too. Teach us to come together in one accord as on the Day of Pentecost.

Show me my sin. Show me any area where I am not walking in unity with the church. Teach me to guard the unity of the church (Acts 2:1). Show me where I am disobeying Your Word. Am I a faithful steward of my time? My talents and gifts? My treasures? Am I faithful with Your truth? Do I share it with others? Am I faithful to the church? Show me, oh, Lord.

Lord, I need Your Holy Spirit to come into my life like a mighty rushing wind, just as You did at Pentecost. I cannot live the Christian life without the Holy Spirit living through me (vv. 2, 4). Pour out Your Spirit, and give me a great awareness of spiritual things. Open my spiritual eyes to see, my spiritual ears to hear, and my mind to understand. Let the fullness of the Holy Spirit be evidenced in my life (vv. 3–4).

Father, send Your cleansing fire upon me. Consume me, fill me with Your Holy Spirit, and transform me (v. 4). Let me speak forth Your Word to whatever group of people I am with. Fill me and use me for Your glory (v. 6).

Thank You. You are glorious and holy, and I praise You. Continue to stir in me a passion to pray, witness, and worship You. Oh, Lord, send revival among Your people. In Jesus' name, amen.

Reflection Questions

1. How do you know for certain you are saved? What evidences or fruits of salvation show in your life?
2. How do you maintain the Holy Spirit's fullness in your life?

3. Do you live under repentance and surrender so that you can be filled with the Holy Spirit daily? How do you pray daily so you will be in a position of surrender to God?

4. We can forfeit the Holy Spirit's filling by not adjusting ourselves to the Word of God. What was the last thing God spoke to you about in His Word? When was that?

5. Are you thirsty for more of God the Holy Spirit? How do you satisfy that thirst?

Chapter 17

REVIVAL under PHILLIP at SAMARIA: Pruning

I am the true vine, and My Father is the vinedresser.
Every branch in Me that does not bear fruit He takes away;
and every branch that bears fruit He prunes, that it may
bear more fruit. (JOHN 15:1–2)

SCRIPTURE:
Acts 8:5–9, 12, 17–21, 26–27

Then Philip went down to the city of Samaria and preached Christ to them. And the multitudes with one accord heeded the things spoken by Philip, hearing and seeing the miracles which he did. For unclean spirits, crying with a loud voice, came out of many who were possessed; and many who were paralyzed and lame were healed. And there was great joy in that city.

But there was a certain man called Simon, who previously practiced sorcery in the city and astonished the people of Samaria, claiming that he was someone great. . . . But when they believed Philip as he preached the things concerning the kingdom of God and the name of Jesus Christ, both men and women were baptized. . . .

Then they laid hands on them, and they received the Holy Spirit.

And when Simon saw that through the laying on of the apostles' hands the Holy Spirit was given, he offered them money, saying, "Give me this power also, that anyone on whom I lay hands may receive the Holy Spirit."

But Peter said to him, "Your money perish with you, because you thought that the gift of God could be purchased with money! You have neither part nor portion in this matter, for your heart is not right in the sight of God. . . ."

Now an angel of the Lord spoke to Philip, saying, "Arise and go toward the south along the road which goes down from Jerusalem to Gaza." This is desert. So he arose and went. And behold, a man of Ethiopia, a eunuch of great authority under Candace the queen of the Ethiopians, who had charge of all her treasury, and had come to Jerusalem to worship.

Spiritual Pruning

As a boy growing up, my dad had grapevines. It was a tiny vineyard consisting of two vines opposite each other, each about ten feet long and growing together over wires. Every year, we enjoyed fresh grapes, grape juice, and homemade grape jelly. At a certain time of the year, my dad would cut back the vines to the point the plants looked horrible. I remember thinking he must be trying to kill them. Dad told me he was merely pruning the vine. What I thought was destruction, as a child, was actually a means of ensuring fruitfulness.

Similarly, spiritual pruning is painful yet absolutely necessary. God prunes us vines, so we will produce good fruit. He prunes fruitful vines, so they will produce even more fruit and bear fruit that will endure: eternal fruit. In John 15, we find God taking us from no fruit, to fruit, to more fruit, to much fruit, to eternal fruit. He does this through the process called pruning. All along the way we must submit, yielding to the pruning of God. The good news is that God always does the pruning, not humans. In times of revival, we will experience the pruning of God and it may be painful, but it is necessary and eternally productive.

In our passage, Philip was being mightily used by God. The Samaritans were responding to the gospel and being saved. Samaritans were the progeny of Jews who had intermarried with Gentiles; they were half-breeds. They were a people rejected by Israel and full-blooded Jews. They could not enter the temple. But the love of God reaches far beyond where religion ceases.

Philip preached to the outcast, the rejected, and the downtrodden. Are you not glad? You were once an outcast, rejected, a misfit, yet the love of God came to you. Are you reaching out to the outcasts around you? We can reach out by treating everyone with respect and by seeking ways to initiate a greeting. Be nice. Always be aware of your surroundings, of who may be listening and watching, and be sensitive to opportunities God initiates.

The church has waited too long for the world to come to us, but God has told us to go to them. In the midst of this great revival, God called Philip to leave and go to the desert. That makes no sense to us as humans. God was using Philip, but now God wanted him to go to the middle of nowhere, a desert. God was pruning Philip.

In pruning, sometimes God allows us to experience good, even great, results. He allows us to bear fruit, but then he prunes us. He takes us or sends us to a desert place where we have no fruit, no past success. God prunes us so that we can bear much more fruit to the glory of God. As a result of this pruning, we can bear eternal fruit. Following by faith and in obedience does not always lead us to where the action is. We may be in perfect obedience although God has led us to a dry, even desert, place. When He asks us to step away from our results, we step away by trusting God.

Getting Personal

In chapter 3, we looked at the revival under Moses and saw how intimately he experienced the presence of God. But before he saw and felt all that glory, Moses was pruned. He is one of greatest examples of God pruning a person for future service. Moses was born at a time when the Egyptians were killing all Hebrew baby boys. His mother put him on the Nile River in a little basket sealed with pitch, so it would not sink. Can you imagine his parents' faith, putting their precious child in that place of danger? Crocodiles, snakes, and other creatures could have killed this helpless baby.

Then the miracle happens; Pharaoh's daughter finds him and decides to raise him as her own son. Then the next miracle: Moses' own mother is brought to nurse and care for him. God's hand is all over this story. We think his path will only be upward from now on. Moses is raised in the palace with all its perks, including the best education and great wealth. He has all the right connections; after all, Pharaoh is his grandfather.

Although Moses was raised in Pharoah's world, he was influenced more by his true, earthly, godly mother who risked her life to give birth to him and protect him. When Moses was grown, we are told in Exodus 2:11, "he went out to his brethren and looked at their burdens." Suddenly, Moses faced a crisis of belief. He must have had conflicting thoughts: *How can I let this continue? What can I do? I'll ignore it and go back to my good life. No, these are my people.*

Facing a Crisis that Demands a Choice

This is how God still works in us today. He gets our attention and forces a crisis of belief that impels us to make a choice. Once we make the first choice, the others choices follow. As God deals with us, He always leads us to the same place, to the cross. We are to live the cross-style life. Paul said it best: "I have been crucified with Christ" (Galatians 2:20). As we choose the cross-style life, that choice will be evident to others.

In Moses' case, he tried to deliver his brethren by killing one Egyptian at a time. This was not God's way. God would have to prune Moses' life more to use him as His deliverer. Moses fled to the back side of the desert and remained there forty years, herding sheep that did not even belong to him. Here Moses lost confidence in his education, his ability, his contacts, and his connections. He realized he was not "all that." As Moses was separated and alone in the desert with sheep, God began to teach him. And all the lessons he learned about shepherding sheep proved useful in the future when he was the shepherd of God's people.

In John 15, in the message of the true Vine, we are told the vine-dresser (God) takes away every branch that does not bear fruit, and every branch that bears fruit He prunes, that it may bear more fruit. The word "takes away" is confusing because it can also be translated "lifts up." Here is the picture. We are growing as a branch along the ground. We have dirt, bugs, and mildew all over us, but our loving heavenly Father comes and lifts us up. He washes us gently, removing the bugs, mildew, and dirt. He lifts us so we can receive more light from the warm sun's rays. He removes any dead branches and those little sucker stems that sprout out and take nourishment away from the main stalk. As we grow, the Father regularly prunes us, cutting back our foliage so our main branch will get the full amount of sap from the vine. What results is that we bear good, plump fruit.

Submitting to Steps in God's Pruning

How will spiritual pruning work with us? Here are the general steps:

1. God gets our attention, forcing a choice.
2. God allows us to try to handle the situation in our own strength.
3. God allows us to fail, so we understand deliverance comes from God, not humans.
4. God separates us from everything we once thought was important and everything that can distract us from Him and His divine purpose.
5. God teaches us lessons we will need to become more useful to Him.

God wants us to depend completely on Him and to bear fruit for His glory. Some lessons we learn quickly, while others may take a lifetime. Time means nothing in God's economy. God just desires that we bear fruit, much fruit, more fruit, and eternal fruit. So He prunes us.

In times of revival, pruning becomes evident. In the revivals I was part of, televisions sat silent. Chores went undone. Vacations were cancelled. Why? People were hungry to commune with God, to read the Word of God, to pray, to unite with others, and to worship. There was a willingness to be still and silent before the Lord, to wait. How could you leave the manifest presence of God? Why would you leave? Time stood still, and all that is important is Christ.

Additional Scripture on Pruning

Ezekiel 36:26; John 15:1–7; James 5:7

Scriptural Prayer for Revival

Persistent Father, remind me that while Philip was doing Your will (preaching Christ), You pruned him. Let me understand pruning comes even as I am being obedient to Your will and calling.

I praise You for Your mighty works and for reaching out to the ignored and downtrodden. I pray that You will burden me to be an intentional witness to all people (Acts 8:5). Father, give me the words to say that will capture the attention of lost people. Move even with miracles, if You so choose (v. 6). I pray You will give me the unction of Your Spirit to witness, to face those who are helpless and hopeless by the world's standards, even those who are possessed by this world and evil spirits. Let physical and spiritual healing and deliverance take place for Your glory (v. 7). As I share with others, let my life show Your glory and joy. Show me how to build relationships, so I can share (v. 8).

Lord, give me a discerning spirit, so I can know the motives and hearts of people, just as You did with Philip (v. 9). Teach me to lay my hands on no person hastily (vv. 17–18). But keep me sensitive to sin and aware and discerning of false teaching and teachers. By Your Holy Spirit, allow me the boldness to challenge them in the name of Your son, Jesus Christ (v. 20). Let counterfeit conversions be exposed for what they are. Move with strong conviction upon individuals who profess to know You, but who live according to the flesh and the desires of this world (vv. 9, 21). Pour out Your Spirit and move mightily, bringing forth repentance (vv. 12, 17).

Father, teach me to understand Your pruning—how You prune

even good fruit, so that eternal fruit may come forth (v. 26). Enable me to be sensitive to Your leading, even when You lead me away from the great outpourings, to go to desert places. Enable me to understand the value of one. Through one, entire families may become open to the gospel and cities and countries may be open to the gospel (vv. 26–27).

Prune my life until I bear fruit only for You. Thank You, Father. You are the one who cuts me back. Oh, Father, send revival to me and to Your people. Be exalted in us and among us. In Jesus' name, amen.

Reflection Questions

1. In what way is your life becoming more narrowed to God's ways? In what ways are you still trying to find fulfillment in the world?

2. Excitement and results can be addictive. How can you guard your life in these areas? What do you need to leave behind, so you can move forward with God?

3. What time robbers, things that distract you from God and His will, are present in your life? What will you do about them?

4. Explain why a good idea may not necessarily be God's will. Explain why an idea that makes no sense may be God's will.

5. What times of pruning, if any, have you experienced? In what ways did those times follow the general steps listed in this chapter?

Chapter 18

REVIVAL under PETER at CAESAREA: Praying

*Continue earnestly in prayer, being vigilant in it with
thanksgiving; meanwhile praying also for us, that God
would open to us a door for the word, to speak the mystery of
Christ, for which I am also in chains.* (COLOSSIANS 4:2–3)

SCRIPTURE:
ACTS 10:9–20

The next day, as they went on their journey and drew near the
city, Peter went up on the housetop to pray, about the sixth hour.
Then he became very hungry and wanted to eat; but while they
made ready, he fell into a trance and saw heaven opened and an
object like a great sheet bound at the four corners, descending
to him and let down to the earth. In it were all kinds of four-foot-
ed animals of the earth, wild beasts, creeping things, and birds of
the air. And a voice came to him, "Rise, Peter; kill and eat."

But Peter said, "Not so, Lord! For I have never eaten anything
common or unclean."

And a voice *spoke* to him again the second time, "What God
has cleansed you must not call common." This was done three
times. And the object was taken up into heaven again.

Now while Peter wondered within himself what this vision which he had seen meant, behold, the men who had been sent from Cornelius had made inquiry for Simon's house, and stood before the gate. And they called and asked whether Simon, whose surname was Peter, was lodging there.

While Peter thought about the vision, the Spirit said to him, "Behold, three men are seeking you. Arise therefore, go down and go with them, doubting nothing; for I have sent them."

Praying

No revival has ever taken place apart from prayer. Only as the message and the messengers are saturated in prayer is the unction of the Holy Spirit poured out. Then words are preached, full of power and life from God. Revival starts in prayer.

A story is told about early African converts to Christianity. They were "earnest and regular in private devotions. Each one reportedly had a separate spot in the thicket where he would pour out his heart to God. Over time, the paths to these places became well worn. As a result, if one of these believers began to neglect prayer, it was soon apparent to the others. They would kindly remind the negligent one, 'Brother, the grass grows on your path.'"[35]

The church is never called a house of preaching or a house of praise, though these things take place. The church is to be known as a house of prayer. Prayer is our lifeline to God. It is the act of breathing spiritual oxygen into our lives. The time you spend in prayer tells you the degree of effectiveness of your spiritual life. Nearly all world religions have some type of prayer. Therefore, we must understand that our prayer is never to be a mere religious routine. Prayer is always based on God's Word and done in faith. For without faith, we cannot even pray correctly. Our faith is not in prayer but in Christ to whom we pray.

Prayer is about coming to God. It is spending time communicating with God, both listening and speaking. Sadhu Sundar Singh was a former Sikh who became a Christian at great risk. He ministered in the Himalayan foothills in the early 1900s and said this about prayer: "The essence of prayer does not consist in asking God for something but in opening our hearts to God, in speaking with Him, and living with Him in perpetual communion. Prayer is continued abandonment to God."[36]

When we have little prayer, we will have little effectiveness. It is amazing the number of things Christians will do rather than pray. Why? Effective prayer is work. It is dependency, obedience, submission, humility, and worship all together. It takes time, effort, and diligence to pray.

Maybe that is why prayer is the crucial ingredient of all true revival. God waits to see how serious we are about seeking Him. In times of prayer, God speaks. He comforts us and confronts us. We will be challenged to depend upon Christ and to wait upon the Lord, even when we have no inclination or human reasoning to do so. That is why prayer is crucial. There will be times God removes all our conscious awareness of His presence, and then our faith must be lived. When we walk with the Lord, we must be prepared to have prejudices, traditions, and wrong beliefs confronted, challenged, and broken down. Pray, do not quit. We are told in Ezekiel 36:37, "Thus says the LORD God: 'I will also let the house of Israel *inquire of Me* to do this for them:'"(emphasis mine). In Joshua 7–9, the failures that Israel experienced in Ai and with the Gibeonites were the direct result of a failure to pray to God. Things are not automatic; we must pray, we must inquire of the Lord, and God will answer in response to our praying.

In this chapter's passage, Cornelius was a devout man who sought God's favor. Through seeking God in ways Cornelius knew and was accustomed to, God led him to Peter and to the place he needed to be to find his true need—to be born again.

For Peter, his time on the rooftop turned into much more as well. While being in a state of prayer and communion with God, Peter was given a clear vision from God that totally turned his traditional thoughts upside down. Peter understood God's vision clearly because he was sensitive and seeking God's will. This encounter transformed Peter's ministry. How important is that principle for us? If we fail to be people whose lives are characterized by prayer, we can miss God's will. That is costly.

Getting Alone with God

God put two totally different men together: one Jewish and the other Gentile; one born again, the other a God-fearer (close, but not yet saved). They were, by tradition, not to associate with each other, much less fellowship together. God broke through tradition and dissolved the barrier. How? He sent a word. He revealed truth. Peter went to a specific place to pray, a place he could be alone without the distractions of life. It was there God spoke.

Likewise, we may need to stop, get alone, pray, and listen for God to speak to us. If we are desperate to hear from God, we must get alone and away from the normal routine of life. We must find a time and place without distractions.

Prejudices and traditions emerge in every life, in individuals and churches. They can go for years unnoticed. Ri Owen Roberts, founder of International Awakening Ministries, warned about the church's love of tradition being at enmity to revival when he said, "Let every church realize that the inordinate love of tradition is a great opponent to revival . . . When a church slays the love of tradition, a major obstacle to revival will be slain with it."[37]

We must have times we seek God in order for Him to break through to us, so we can see these hindrances. We should not be surprised when Jesus challenges our traditional viewpoint or understanding that is not scriptural.

Is there any prejudice you hold to that God is asking you to release? God is no respecter of persons. God is completely impartial and wants all to be saved, so revival can be no respecter of persons. Leonard Ravenhill said it well when he said, "No man is greater than his prayer life."[38] Revival starts in prayer.

Getting Personal

In the forty-day revival I described earlier, I think I never truly witnessed such a time of unrelenting prayer. We, as a church body, began praying personally and corporately weeks prior to the revival. We opened the first service in prayer, and from that point forward we prayed earnestly for forty days. You could hear the prayers. You could feel the prayers. We also accompanied our prayers with fasting. We all witnessed the unleashing of God's power in response to those heartfelt prayers.

People prayed all types of prayers: prayers of thanksgiving, praise, confession, restoration. They asked for all sorts of things: submission to His will, guidance and direction, double portions of the Holy Spirit, wisdom. They prayed for all sorts of things for others: protection from evil, deliverance from addictions. There were prayers of adoration and prayers of humble silence and so many more.

Prevailing prayer was everywhere. To prevail with God in prayer, the *pray-er* must have an attitude of submission and humility before God. Brokenness must be the characteristic of this person's life. The only way we can be receptive and responsive to whatever God wants to do in our lives or as a church is to yield completely and allow our hearts to be sensitive to the Holy Spirit's touch and leading.

When the heavens opened and it was evident that God was reigning over our church, a few moments or even a few hours of prayer a day became insufficient. Our greatest desire was to maintain the intimate connection we were experiencing with our Father, and prayer was our greatest means of doing so.

How vital were those prayers to the overall revival experience? I believe it was these deep, heartfelt prayers that continued to fuel His power and presence. Prayer plunged us into an even deeper, more intimate relationship with Him. Because of these prayers, God allowed us the glory of experiencing an open stairway to heaven.

Are you thinking about your church or gathering and wishing for a similar experience? Remember Leonard Ravenhill's words: "Without exception, all true revivals of the past began after years of agonizing, hell-robbing, earth-shaking, heaven-sent intercession. The secret to true revival in our day is still the same. But where, oh where are the intercessors?"[39]

You can be that one intercessor who prays and starts a revival.

Additional Scripture on Praying

1 Kings 8:54; 2 Chronicles 6:19–20, 7:15; Matthew 21:22; Acts 1:14; Ephesians 6:18; Colossians 4:2

Scriptural Prayer for Revival

Mighty God, give me the burden for prayer so that revival may come. Just as You moved on Peter, move on me as I pray. Let me have a specific time and place to go to You in prayer. Prompt me throughout the day to seek You in prayer. Teach me to pray—to pray with travail, with a burden. I do not merely seek revival, but I long for the great Reviver (Acts 10:9).

As I pray, Lord, bring to my mind things, beliefs, and practices that are not right. Teach me to unlearn things that I may have accepted as true, but You tell me they are not (vv. 10–13). Teach me the difference between clean and unclean, between holy and what is unholy. Teach me Your ways. Forgive me, Lord, for those times I have allowed things to have priority over You. Enable me to press through the distractions of life and not forfeit my time with You (v. 15). Speak to me through Your Word, through Your Holy Spirit, through dreams or visions. Challenge me; change me into Your image, just as You did with Peter. Show me how to process Your truth and apply it to my life. Oh God, let me recognize Your voice (vv. 10, 13, 15, 19).

Lord, teach me never to say no to You, for if I say no to You, then You are no longer my Lord. As I process truth, be patient with me (v. 14).

Father, teach me the importance of thinking about and meditating on Your Word. Confront and convict and challenge and comfort me with Your Word. (v. 19). Let me be sensitive to Your Spirit when You speak to me. Let me rise and walk in obedience to Your leading, doubting nothing (v. 20).

Please, Lord, send revival. Let us recognize when You are trying to change us, so that we may know Your reviving. Teach me, oh Lord, to pray through for revival. In Jesus' name, amen.

Reflection Questions

1. Do you have a regular time and place to pray? If so, where and when do you pray?

2. When you pray, how much of your prayer is about you and yours? How frequently do you lift others to God in prayer? Do you feel a burden to pray for others? If not, why not? What is your prayer burden?

3. When you pray, how much time do you spend listening for God to speak? How does He speak to you? What was the last thing God told you in prayer?

4. Do you pray God's will be done in a situation, or do you ask God to do your will? How do you know the difference?

5. How do you relate what is happening in your everyday life to your prayers?

6. What is God saying to you right now?

Chapter 19

REVIVAL under PAUL and SILAS in EUROPE: Exercising Faith

So then faith comes by hearing, and hearing by the word of God. (ROMANS 10:17)

SCRIPTURE:
1 THESSALONIANS 1:2–10

We give thanks to God always for you all, making mention of you in our prayers, remembering without ceasing your work of faith, labor of love, and patience of hope in our Lord Jesus Christ in the sight of our God and Father, knowing, beloved brethren, your election by God. For our gospel did not come to you in word only, but also in power, and in the Holy Spirit and in much assurance, as you know what kind of men we were among you for your sake.

And you became followers of us and of the Lord, having received the word in much affliction, with joy of the Holy Spirit, so that you became examples to all in Macedonia and Achaia who believe. For from you the word of the Lord has sounded forth, not only in Macedonia and Achaia, but also in every place. Your faith toward God has gone out, so that we do not need to say anything. For they themselves declare concerning us what manner of entry we had to you, and how you turned to God from idols to serve the living and true God, and to wait for His Son from heaven, whom He raised from the dead, *even* Jesus who delivers us from the wrath to come.

Exercising Faith

One night, a house caught fire and a young boy was forced to flee to the roof. His father, knowing the boy was in danger, stood on the ground below with outstretched arms, calling to his son, "Jump! I'll catch you."

All the boy could see, however, was flames, smoke, and blackness. He was afraid to leave the roof.

His father kept yelling, "Jump! I'll catch you."

The boy protested, "Daddy, I can't see you."

"But I can see you," the father said, "and that's all that matters."

So the boy jumped, and his father caught him safely.

The boy expressed a faith that responded to the words of his father. Oh, that we would have such a faith that responds to the words and voice of our heavenly Father.

The Bible says faith comes by hearing and hearing comes through the Word of God. God takes His Word, speaks it to my mind and spirit. He quickens the Word specifically to me and it becomes real. Then, I must respond to the Word that He has made alive. That is faith, my responding to the living Word of God. If I do not respond in agreement and obedience, then I do not have faith. Faith itself is a gift to us from God for the purpose of believing unto salvation, and then releasing the promises of God in our lives. Faith becomes real as we respond to God in humble obedience. We obey with our actions and with an attitude of agreement that God's will is best. God could force us to obey, but that is not what He wants. God wants our obedience to flow willingly from a surrendered heart. That is an attitude of agreement.

In Hebrews 3:19, we are told that the children of Israel who wandered in the desert for forty years "could not enter in [to the Promised Land] because of unbelief." When we hear God's Word and we ignore it, we live in Unbelief Land. There is no neutral ground. To ignore the Word of God is a denial of our faith, and from that moment, our faith begins to diminish. In seasons of revival, our faith is challenged and stretched, all for the purpose of glorifying God.

Saving faith begins with an understanding; it is recognition of God's truth. Faith is the unqualified acceptance of and exclusive dependency upon Jesus Christ. It has an intellectual element, an emotional element, and a volitional element. The intellectual element is where we give conscious awareness or assent to the truth of God as the Holy Spirit opens our minds. Thus, we engage our minds to God's Word. The emotional element is when we want it for ourselves; we desire it. Again, the Holy Spirit gives us the desire for God. These two elements alone, however, are not enough to bring salvation. The third element, the volition, our will, must be involved so that we choose to surrender to Christ and His will. As the Holy Spirit enables you to surrender in this fashion, salvation takes place. Saving faith results when you yield your will to Christ. True saving faith enables you to abide in Christ and walk victoriously.

Paul must have felt like a parent to the church of the Thessalonians. The believers' faith, hope, love, and perseverance in the face of persecution were exemplary. Paul encouraged them to continue in their faith, to increase in their love for one another, to rejoice, to pray, and to give thanks always.

We also need that kind of encouragement amidst a hostile society. We live in a land where tolerance is everything, so we need to hear, "Press on, don't stop, don't look back, and keep going." How do we press on? We press on by rejoicing always, by praying without ceasing, and by being thankful in all things. We press on by faith. When God burns His Word in your heart, live it. Live by faith in God, in God's Word; adjust your life to it. Genuine faith inevitably results in a life of obedience to God and His Word. This willful obedience to His Word not only enables our faith to develop but also pleases God and displays our living testimony to the world where we live.

When was the last time you thanked God for your difficulties, knowing they were working faith in you? Have you rejoiced in your trials, knowing they were conforming you to the image of Christ?

Getting Personal

As we daily abide in the Word of God and prayer, our faith develops. There will be a time when we face a crisis of belief (a moment of decision), and we have to decide if we will obey God regardless of the outcome. Will we choose the way of God or the world?

When the voice of God speaks to our minds and spirits, we must deliberately choose to obey. As God calls us to obey, He enables us to obey. That is the beauty of it all. He prepares us in advance by His Word and His Spirit for whatever we need to do to obey. The way of the cross must be followed, resulting in self-denial. God's commands are God's enablement for us to obey Him.

God always gives faith to obey, but in the times of revival I have witnessed, it appears He gives a greater enduement to obey. In my congregation, men and women, by faith, stood before the group and confessed their sins. No one asked them to confess, but they had to obey God. The confessions were humiliating and painful, but as they obeyed God, God enabled them and they were delivered to freedom. They were no longer in bondage, no longer in shame. They were free in Christ.

After one man was restored, he said God told him to go and witness in a local department store. He left the service. Around nine p.m., he walked into the store, stood in front of the checkout lines, and shouted as loud as he could: "God is visiting Indiana Avenue Church. Don't miss it." Then he left and returned to the service. Sounds silly, but for him, he obeyed and acted in faith.

Now and then, other people had to obey God in faith, leaving the service and going to someone they had offended and asking forgiveness. Why? God's Word tells us to interrupt worship, the most important thing we are to be about, and go seek to restore an offended brother (Matthew 5:24). When the Word of God comes to you, God is speaking. But only as you obey the Word is your faith activated.

One children's Sunday school teacher had been a smoker for twenty-one years. For the past five years she had been a closet smoker; few people knew and that is how she wanted it. During revival, God convicted her and she stood and confessed her sin to the entire church and asked for prayer to overcome the habit. She made it through the first day, but on the second day the battle came. She called me and others, crying and saying, "I can't do this. Please pray for me. Please pray!" Moment by moment, God gave her victory as she called out to Him and surrounded herself with intercessors for her need. Her faith was weak and struggling, but her faith was also active, calling out to God. God answered her with deliverance. Over time, He removed her craving and the entire addiction.

When we fail to respond to the voice of God and the conviction of the Holy Spirit, we enter unbelief. Unbelief is where many people exist. They never know the fullness of life Christ offers because that requires faith. In revival, our faith is challenged, refreshed, and exemplified.

Additional Scripture on Exercising Faith

Deuteronomy 32:20; Habakkuk 2:4; Matthew 9:2, 21:21; Romans 10:17; Ephesians 2:8–9

Scriptural Prayer for Revival

Gentle Father, faith comes as Your Word is quickened in me and I respond in obedience. Let me always respond quickly to Your Word. Thank You for the gift of faith, for my faith. Let my faith grow so that when revival comes, I am ready and available (1 Thessalonians 1:2).

Father, allow my faith to grow and develop, so that it may be effective unto Your glory. Teach me to persevere in faith amidst opposition and persecution. Let love flow through my life and my local church, and let us understand that love is a labor. Let us be faithful in Your Word by the power of the Holy Spirit (v. 3).

Your Word says in Romans 14:23, "Whatever is not of faith is sin." Let this sin of unfaithfulness not be found in me or Your church. Expose it. Cleanse and wash me from every stain of sin. Father, we need revival. We need You to move in us and through us, so a lost world will see unity and be drawn to You. Father, allow Your Word to flow in power and the anointing of the Holy Spirit (v. 5).

Lord, I need You to move in me. Teach me how to receive Your Word even in affliction, but with joy. Let me truly understand that suffering for You is a grace gift (v. 6).

Oh Lord, show me how to be an example of faith to others (v. 7). Let my faith go out from city to city (v. 8). Let us hear the testimonies of others, how they have turned from darkness to Your glorious light and are serving You (v. 9).

Send revival, Lord. Begin in me. Keep my hope strong in You. Come, Lord Jesus. We wait for You (v. 10). In the name of Jesus, amen.

Reflection Questions

1. For faith to be expectant, it must be active and guided by the truth of God's Word. When you go to church, are you expecting to meet God? Are you expecting God to move? If so, how? What is your faith expecting God to do?

2. How do you regularly feed your faith? In what ways do you feed your flesh? How have you seen your faith increase?

3. How do you add to your faith virtue, knowledge, self-control, perseverance, godliness, brotherly kindness and love? (2 Peter 1:5–7). Be specific.

4. If you are more oriented to the world than to Christ and His kingdom, then you are not expressing faith. How are you, or how can you be, more oriented to Christ than the world?

Chapter 20

PREVAILING with GOD FOR REVIVAL: Waiting

*But those who wait on the L*ORD *shall renew their strength;*
They shall mount up with wings like eagles, They shall run
and not be weary, They shall walk and not faint.

(ISAIAH 40:31)

SCRIPTURE:
LUKE 24:44–53

Then He said to them, "These *are* the words which I spoke to you while I was still with you, that all things must be fulfilled which were written in the Law of Moses and *the* Prophets and *the* Psalms concerning Me." And He opened their understanding, that they might comprehend the Scriptures.

Then He said to them, "Thus it is written, and thus it was necessary for the Christ to suffer and to rise from the dead the third day, and that repentance and remission of sins should be preached in His name to all nations, beginning at Jerusalem. And you are witnesses of these things. Behold, I send the Promise of My Father upon you; but tarry in the city of Jerusalem until you are endued with power from on high."

And He led them out as far as Bethany, and He lifted up His hands and blessed them. Now it came to pass, while He blessed them, that He was parted from them and carried up into heaven. And they worshiped Him, and returned to Jerusalem with great joy, and were continually in the temple praising and blessing God. Amen.

Waiting on God

Waiting. We may not like it, but we have all had to learn to wait. Waiting on the Lord is a test to see how desperate we are for God. It is a challenging yet indispensable element in revival. G. Campbell Morgan, minister in the late 1800s and early 1900s, said, "Waiting for God is not laziness. Waiting for God is not going to sleep. Waiting for God is not the abandonment of effort. Waiting for God means: first, activity under command; second, readiness for any new command that may come; third, the ability to do nothing until the command is given."[40]

Waiting on the Lord does not mean we sit and do nothing. Waiting upon the Lord is a positive, deliberate choice we make. It is active and aggressive. It demands strength, courage, faith, and trust in God. When we wait upon the Lord, we submit our will to God's will. We pause for further instruction and direction from the Master. While we wait, we continue doing the last thing God told us to do. We continue seeking God through His Word and prayer. As we wait, we are to be restfully available. But when God speaks, we are to be instantly obedient. Much of our lives may be spent waiting.

In Luke 24, Jesus had been crucified, buried, and resurrected. He soon would ascend and be exalted to the right hand of the Father. For forty days, he taught His disciples and guided them in truth. He opened Scripture to them and gave them understanding. That is what we need today, for Jesus to open Scripture to us, so we can have understanding. On our own, we cannot understand the Scriptures or truths of God.

Realize it or not, we are utterly dependent on the Holy Spirit to teach us. We have to learn to tarry, to wait, not just five minutes or one hour, but wait ten days if need be or longer. To tarry is to persevere in faith. For the disciples, they were to tarry in Jerusalem, a place of hostility, death, and adversity. Unless we learn to tarry, we will never experience the power from on high, the dynamite power of the Holy Spirit who enables us to witness, minister, and continue. Have you learned to wait before God?

Getting Personal

I can tell you the exact location where God placed revival in my heart. My wife and I attended a Prayer for Spiritual Awakening Conference at the Grace Baptist Church in Parkersburg, West Virginia. In the fall of 1989, a man named Henry Blackaby was leading and Robert E. Coleman was present to bear testimony of the revival that took place on the Asbury College campus in 1970.

God began to stir in me a longing for genuine revival. Later, I was given a copy of the *Experiencing God* workbook by Henry Blackaby and Claude King. The person who gave it to me made me promise I would do only one day at a time. I did as she asked, but I devoured the book. I longed for revival, and I prayed for it. I was hungry for more of God and His presence.

For years, I prayed and read everything I could on true revival. And I waited. I saw and experienced glimpses of His glory. In some meetings, the group would receive a taste of heaven, but I continued to pray and wait.

When I came to Indiana Avenue Church in 1993, I did not come to a great situation. I did not come to a good situation. I came to a dead situation. The only thing attractive about the church was the people's desperation. I knew this was where God was leading me.

The church was located in a small, rural, mountainous area in east Tennessee. There were about seventy-five people in attendance when I first came. The town's population was about eight thousand, with a surrounding population of about seventeen thousand. There were no mega-churches in the area, but there were more than one hundred churches. My church was predominately older people, and my wife and I were both thirty-two years old. We loved our people. We prayed, served, and waited on God to move. We waited five years before the church turned the corner, and we felt like we would survive.

After we had been there nine years, things were going smoothly. People were being saved. Attendance was up and finances were holding steady. We had no debts, and there was an excitement and expectancy in the church. My wife and I still prayed for revival, and we waited.

Resisting the Devil

About this time, the devil began to stir greatly in our church. We had the normal issues all along, but at year number nine, "all hell broke loose." I was falsely accused regarding the church finances. Some of the members got it in their minds that I was doing things wrong. When a number of people have a confidence problem with the pastor, everything stops. For an entire year, no new people became members and no one was baptized. We had few visitors. It was awful. I stood before the congregation and explained everything they wanted to know and assured them that I had done nothing wrong. I begged God to release me from this place, but He would not.

Finally, the church hired an outside auditor to review all the financial records. Their conclusion: I had done nothing wrong, but the financial secretary had made many mistakes in her bookkeeping.

You would think after nine years of pastoring and visiting the sick in hospitals, nine years of preaching, praying, and seeking God, this would not happen, but it did. Was it right? No. Yet God had allowed it. He is sovereign, and He is in control. My wife and I had to process it and respond to in faith. We came forth from it stronger, and we have no bitterness. I was frustrated and upset many times, but I had no bitterness. I wanted to run away, but God said, "No." So we prayed and we waited on God to vindicate us, and in time, He did.

Persevering through All

No one would have blamed us for leaving; after all, we were being falsely accused. When do sheep need shepherding and leadership? In the hard, difficult times, more so than the good times. Many pastors leave in the hard times. Sheep will be sheep, and they are prone to wander as well as bite. We are called to shepherd the flock of God in good times and not so good of times.

Had my wife and I chosen to leave, look what we would have missed: a revival in Florida that was amazing and where my kids accepted Christ and a revival in Tennessee that lasted forty days, continued for eleven months, and transitioned and transformed my ministry.

You and I have to learn to wait on the Lord. Every situation in life has its own set of trials and challenges; we must learn to wait on the Lord. Sometimes it is not fun, but it is crucial to your spiritual life. I am no expert, but I do know when God says, "No." I know when all of heaven is silent, God is saying, "Wait." If we refuse either of those commands, we can miss God.

Revival occurs when the God of glory draws close to us, and we know His presence. Once you have tasted the manifest presence of God, it spoils you. You know when you have experienced it, and you know when you have come short. Revival leaves you constantly longing for more and more of God. So we pray, we wait, and we remain faithful. In God's time, He will send personal revival. If we fail to wait and obey God, we can miss it. If we wait patiently, the Great Reviver *will* send revival. Learn to wait upon the Lord and He will answer.

Additional Scripture on Waiting

Psalm 37:9, 40:1, 46:10–11; Isaiah 8:17; 40:31

Scriptural Prayer for Revival

All Sufficient Father, as the disciples waited for You in Jerusalem, I wait for You. Give me renewed strength to wait. Fulfill Your Word in my life and in the church for revival's sake (Luke 24:44).

Father, I need You to open my understanding so I can comprehend Scripture. Your Word is truth. Give me understanding as You did the disciples in Jerusalem (v. 45). I bow before You, Lord, waiting on Your moving, Your leading, and Your presence. Teach me the importance of waiting in the places You have chosen for me (v. 49). Teach me how to wait with hope and understanding (vv. 45, 49).

Oh, Father, I get in a hurry and try to rush in and out of Your presence. I try to manipulate You to my schedule and my plans. Father, forgive me of this sin. Your last word was for us to preach repentance for the remission of sin. Let me be faithful to that command. Burn in me the importance of sharing Your Word and not the opinions of man (v. 47). May I be a witness of Your Word and Your power (v. 48).

Teach me to adjust myself to You, to tarry until You speak and direct. Oh, Father, I need Your power day by day, moment by moment. Keep me hungering and thirsting after You (v. 49). Teach me how not to fill myself with things that will not satisfy. How my flesh craves the world! Deliver me. I know only You can satisfy. The world may pacify me, but You, Lord, truly satisfy my soul. Teach me how to fill my mind, my heart, my time with You and Your Word.

Father, let me worship You, even in difficult times and places (v. 52). Let Your blessings flow forth from Your throne (v. 51). Let them be evidence to all that I, we, have been in Your presence. Fill me with great joy (v. 52). Let me understand the need I have to be together with Your people, the church, praising and blessing Your name (v. 53).

Father, send revival. We wait before You. In the name of Jesus, amen.

Reflection Questions

1. Many times when we wait, all we hear is silence. What is your response to God when that happens?

2. How is waiting on God not inactivity?

3. If we fail to wait on God, we miss God and His power and plan. If we fail to wait on God, we will miss God's best. Understanding that, what do you see as God's plan for you right now? How has God's power been demonstrated in your life to fulfill His plan?

4. As we wait on God, He shows us areas of impatience and doubt. What specifically has He shown you in these areas?

5. What does it mean to wait with expectancy? How do you keep expectancy strong?

Chapter 21

PREPARING for PERSONAL REVIVAL: Practicing Humility

And whoever exalts himself will be humbled, and he who humbles himself will be exalted. (Matthew 23:12)

SCRIPTURE:
JAMES 4:1–4, 6–11

Where do wars and fights *come* from among you? Do *they* not come from your *desires for* pleasure that war in your members? You lust and do not have. You murder and covet and cannot obtain. You fight and war. Yet you do not have because you do not ask. You ask and do not receive, because you ask amiss, that you may spend *it* on your pleasures. Adulterers and adulteresses! Do you not know that friendship with the world is enmity with God? Whoever therefore wants to be a friend of the world makes himself an enemy of God. . . .

But He gives more grace. Therefore He says: "God resists the proud, But gives grace to the humble."

Therefore submit to God. Resist the devil and he will flee from you. Draw near to God and He will draw near to you. Cleanse *your* hands, *you* sinners; and purify *your* hearts, *you* double-minded. Lament and mourn and weep! Let your laughter be turned to mourning and *your* joy to gloom. Humble yourselves in the sight of the Lord, and He will lift you up.

Do not speak evil of one another, brethren. He who speaks evil of a brother and judges his brother, speaks evil of the law and judges the law. But if you judge the law, you are not a doer of the law but a judge.

Practicing Humility

In the most famous passage on revival, 2 Chronicles 7:14, we are told to humble ourselves and pray. Humility is the first requirement for revival. If you refuse to humble yourself, you will not even pray correctly. Humbling yourself is crucial for revival. It is an act of submission to the lordship of Jesus Christ. It is an act of surrender of our rights unto God. It is an act of faith and obedience to the Spirit. The end result will be submission to others.

William Temple, Archbishop of Canterbury during World War 2, said, "Humility does not mean thinking less of yourself than of other people, nor does it mean having a low opinion of your own gifts. It means freedom from thinking about yourself one way or the other at all."[41] In the world today, there is a unity crisis, because there is a scarcity of humility. With a scarcity of humility comes an overabundance of pride. Pride makes it difficult for people to work together because everyone does what is right in his or her own eyes. Everyone wants to be the boss, and no one wants to be the worker. One of the primary reasons marriages fail today is the lack of humility between spouses. Churches also have internal struggles because of the lack of humility. One of our greatest needs is humility.

What does it mean to be humble? In the Greek, it means "being of lowly estate" and "seeing others as higher than our self." The Greek word *tapeinoo* literally means "to level a mountain, or a hill." Humble people are those who have no hills sticking up. They are not filled up with hot air of arrogance and pride.

If we are not daily practicing humility, then we are not close to personal revival. Not to be practicing humility means we are exhibiting pride, and God hates pride. James 4:6 says, "God resists the proud, but gives grace to the humble." The Bible commands us to humble ourselves. How do you humble yourself? Humility is a choice. You can choose to be humble, or you can let God humble you. Choosing to be humble is the right way.

Submitting in act and attitude to God is how we humble ourselves before God. We submit our lives and our lifestyle to God's Word and will. Therefore, I submit to God my time, resources, finances, talents, and abilities. Humility to God will be evidenced as I submit myself to the leadership He has established in my local church. "Obey those who rule over you, and be submissive, for they watch out for your souls, as those who must give account. Let them do so with joy and not with grief, for that would be unprofitable for you" (Hebrews 13:17). As I humble myself, my attitude is to be that of thankfulness and joy. I am faithful to the body of Christ, the local church, and I am available for service to it. We cannot submit to God and humble ourselves before Him without adjusting our lives to Scripture. A person cannot pick and choose how he or she obeys God. We cannot serve our churches at our own convenience and at the same time be submissive and humble before God.

True humility responds to divine instruction and then obeys. False humility takes the humble posture of submission but does not obey. James 4 shows us two sins that destroy humility. One is in the use of your speech to speak evil, or speaking evil against others and being judgmental (James 4:11). You think you are better than others.

The other is arrogance, meaning you have a boastful or arrogant spirit (James 4:13–16). Again, you think you are better than others.

When humility is not in your life, then you cannot approach God or worship God, and revival will not come. Submission to God is the act of humbling ourselves to God. When we humble ourselves, God will exalt us. Yet even when God exalts us, it is for His glory. When God humbles us, however, we will be humiliated. Humiliation or humbling ourselves, that is our choice.

When we willingly submit to God by faith, the Bible promises that the devil will flee from us. If the devil is not fleeing from you, then ask yourself if you are truly submitting to God. Is there an area of your life that you are withholding from Christ Jesus? Revival demands humility.

Getting Personal

When God was moving, our church met every day for forty days in continuous revival services. Bringing the everyday services to an end was so difficult. The closest thing I can compare it with is when a person goes on an extended fast, and for days and weeks he or she chooses to seek God rather than to eat. Bringing a fast of extended duration to an end is hard, but you must or eventually you will die. When you stop the fast, you get a feeling of a loss of intimacy.

To end our consecutive meetings, I had to hear from God. After forty days, I knew we had fulfilled what God wanted. I knew it in my spirit because, since day twenty-one, I had sought God's will about how and when to close the meeting.

God impressed on me that we were to have a foot washing service. I did not announce this in advance, since it was not a typical practice for the church, although it is scriptural. I placed twenty tubs around the altar area, along with towels. Then I explained what we were about to do. I read the passage in John 13 about Jesus washing the disciples' feet. I requested only that should people choose to take part, they were simply to ask God whose feet they were to wash. I instructed them to ask that person's permission first. If the person agreed, then while they washed that person's feet, I asked them to pray for that person.

After a season of prayer at the altar, people began to go and wash the feet of others. Everyone participated. Husbands washed their wives' feet, and wives washed their husband's feet. Manly men stooped down and took the feet of other men and washed them. Many people came to wash my feet. Surprisingly, I discovered it was easier for me to wash someone else's feet than to have my feet washed. Why? Pride. It is always easier to do for others than to have someone do for you. That is the great danger of doing things; pride can creep in. I had to repent of my pride. I thanked God for showing me, and I asked His forgiveness.

One man and his family had attended nearly every service. They were poor, wore ragged clothes, and often had a bad odor. I watched as one of the godliest men in our church, who was also a successful businessman in the community, went to this ragged man. I watched as he asked if he could wash his feet, and I watched as he removed the man's shoes and socks. I was amazed. I kept watching as he washed the feet of this poor, dirty, and smelly man and prayed over him. God used that scene to smite my heart, saying, "Why haven't you done this for him?" I wept as I obeyed God.

Jesus wants to wash our feet. Just as I want to resist others from washing my feet, I can resist Christ from washing me. The only way we will ever be humble before God is when we live humbly before others. Only as we live in humility do we release Christ in our lives to minister through us.

Do not let revival take place around you and allow yourself to miss it. Let revival take place in you, too. Humble yourself, pray, seek God's face, and turn from anything that is not becoming of Christ. God will hear and answer, and revival will come.

Additional Scripture on Practicing Humility

Leviticus 26:40–41; Proverbs 16:19, 29:23; Isaiah 57:15; Matthew 18:4; 1 Peter 5:5–6

Scriptural Prayer for Revival

Ever Present Father, I come before You seeking You to move in revival among Your people. Teach me, now, to be still and wait upon You. Show me with clarity how much of my life is given to seeking pleasures. Show me any addiction to good times that I have (James 4:1–3). Lord, am I a friend of the world? Am I more concerned with my social activities than spending time seeking and serving You (v. 4)?

Father, daily I must put off pride and choose to live in humility. Let me recognize the opportunities You send to practice humility, especially with my spouse (v. 6).

Expose in me any area I am not in submission to You. Bring to my mind ways I am living in disobedience to Your Word. Allow me to bring all that I am before You this day. Father, enable me to be wise to the methods of the devil and to resist him in faith. Show me how my resisting is always connected by submission to You and Your Word (v. 7).

Do not allow me to rest when I give the devil room or access to my life. Expose my pride. Let me understand how much You hate pride and resist the proud. Cleanse me of my pride—pride of ability, appearance, accomplishment, family, and possessions (v. 6).

Wash me, Lord. Let me come before You with clean hands, outwardly being right with You, and a clean heart, inwardly being right in my motives. Fill me afresh with Your Holy Spirit, and let me reflect You. Let me know Your exaltation. Let me glory in You (v. 8).

Father, I pray for revival. You have promised in Your Word, "If [we] will humble ourselves and pray," You will answer. Lord, let Your church understand the necessity of humility. Let us understand the desperate need of the hour. May I humble myself and call out to You to come in revival (v. 10). Let brokenness be manifest in me and in Your people. Oh Lord, we need You this hour, this moment. Come, Lord, in revival power. Cleanse us and make us anew. In Jesus' name, amen.

Reflection Questions

1. What specific actions have you taken to humble yourself before God?
2. When was the last time you admitted your weaknesses or failures to someone else? To whom did you confess, and what did you share?
3. In what ways are you tempted to receive the applause of the world, of others?
4. How is Christ glorified in your life?
5. Humility is a choice we must make every day. What are some ways you can be sure you practice humility with others? In your speech? In your driving? With your spouse?
6. What is God saying to you today?

Endnotes

1. Del Fehsenfeld Jr., *Ablaze with His Glory* (Nashville: Thomas Nelson, 1993), 189–190.

2. Gypsy Smith quoted at Simon Guillebaud Blog, May 9, 2012. Accessed March 1, 2013. http://www.simonguillebaud.com/blog/1-general/98-revival-praying-and-chalk-circles.

3. David Smithers, "William C. Burns," Awake and Go! Global Prayer Network. Accessed February 28, 2013. http://www.watchword.org/index.php?option=com_content&task=view&id=18.

4. *USA Today*, Oct. 24, 1997, quoted at Sermon Central. Accessed February 25, 2013. http://www.sermoncentral.com/illustrations/statistics-about-jesus-and-money.asp.

5. Ted S. Rendall quoted at Sermon Index. Accessed February 26, 2013. http://www.sermonindex.net/modules/newbb/viewtopic.php?topic_id=18969&forum=16&0.

6. G. Campbell Morgan quoted at OChristian.com, "Christian Quotes." Accessed February 28, 2013. http://christian-quotes.ochristian.com/G.-Campbell-Morgan-Quotes/page-2.shtml.

7. Marvin R. Vincent, *Vincent's Word Studies of the New Testament,* vol. 2 (Mclean, VA: Macdonald Publishing), 320.

8. E. M. Bounds quoted in LiftUpUSA.com, "Revival/Awakening," added June 13, 2004. Accessed May 27, 2009. www.liftupusa.com/revival.html.

9. *Foxe: Voices of the Martyrs: 33 AD to Today* (Alachua, FL: Bridge-Logos and Voice of the Martyrs, March 2007), 51.

10. J. Vernon McGee quoted at OChristian.com, "Christian Articles," "Behind the Black Curtain in the Upper Room." Accessed March 4, 2013. http://articles.ochristian.com/article15588.shtml.

11. Michael Catt, *The Power of Desperation* (Nashville: B&H Publishing, 2009), 97–98.

12. D. L. Moody quoted at OChristian.com, "Christian Quotes," "D. L. Moody on Prayer." Accessed February 22, 2013. http://christian-quotes.ochristian.com/christian-quotes_ochristian.cgi?find=Christian-quotes-by-D.L.+Moody-on-Prayer.

13. R. A. Torrey quoted at OChristian.com, "Christian Quotes." Accessed February 28, 2013. http://christian-quotes.ochristian.com/R.A.-Torrey-Quotes/.

14. Jeff Strite, "Laying It on the Altar," added March 2, 2009, p. 2. Accessed February 21, 2013. http://www.sermoncentral.com/sermons/laying-it-on-the-altar-jeff-strite-sermon-on-sacrifices-133091.asp.

15. Seth Joshua quoted in David Smithers, "John Hyde," Awake and Go! Global Prayer Network. Accessed February 22, 2013. http://www.watchword.org/index.php?option=com_content&task=view&id=28.

16. *Our Daily Bread* quoted at Sermon Illustrations, "Sanctification." Accessed February 28, 2013. http://www.sermonillustrations.com/a-z/s/sanctification.htm.

17. Gordon MacDonald, *Ordering Your Private World*, (Nashville: Thomas Nelson, 2003), 233–234.

18. Wellington Boone quoted at Lift Up USA, "Revival Awakening." Accessed Feb. 22, 2013. www.liftupusa.com/revival.html.

19. Oswald Chambers quoted at Daily Christian Quote, November 16, 2011. Accessed Feb. 22, 2013. http://dailychristianquote.com/dcqchambers.html.

20. Ole S. Hallesby, *Prayer* (Minneapolis: Augsburg Publishing House, 1994), 112.

21. J. R. W. Stott, *Between Two Worlds* (Grand Rapids: Eerdmans, 1982), 270.

22. Michael Catt, *The Power of Persistence* (Nashville: B&H Publishing, 2009), 54.

23. Oswald J. Smith quoted at Sermon Illustrations. Accessed February 22, 2013. http://www.sermonillustrations.com/a-z/p/preaching.htm.

24. David Wilkerson, "When Judgment Becomes Evident," You Tube. Uploaded Mar. 4, 2009. Accessed May 10, 2011. http://www.youtube.com/watch?v=KeVzyDU7_-I.

25. Richard Owen Roberts, *Revival Commentary,* vol. 2, no. 2, (Wheaton, IL: International Awakening Ministries, 1997), 5.

26. Arthur Wallis, *In the Day of Thy Power* (London: Christian Literature Crusade, 1956), 81.

27. Roy Hession, *The Calvary Road* (London: Christian Literature Crusade, 1950), 21.

28. Sandra Cain, unpublished testimony written and given to the author about events that occurred in the 2006 revival in LaFollette, TN.

29. Mordecia Ham quoted in David Smithers, "Mordecai Ham," Awake and Go! Global Prayer Network. Accessed Feb. 26, 2013. http://www.watchword.org/index.php?option=com_content&task=view&id=27.

30. Patrick Morley quoted at Sermon Illustrations, "Repentance," "C. Swindoll, *John the Baptizer,* Bible Study Guide, p. 16." Accessed March 4, 2013. http://www.sermonillustrations.com/a-z/r/repentance.htm.

31. D. L. Moody quoted in J. Kuhatschek, *Taking the Guesswork Out of Applying the Bible* (Westmont, IL: Intervarsity Press, 1990), 153ff.

32. D. L. Moody quoted in John R. Rice, *How Great Soul Winners Were Filled with the Holy Spirit* (Murfreesboro, TN: Sword of the Lord Publishers, 1949), 4–5.

33. Evan Roberts quoted in Oswald J. Smith, *The Revival We Need* (London and Edinburgh: Marshall, Morgan and Scott, 1932), 42–44.

34. F. B. Meyers quoted in John Charles Pollock with Ian Randall, *The*

Keswick Story (Fort Washington, PA: Christian Literature Crusade Publications, 2006), 138–139.

35. Sermon Illustrations, "Prayer," quoted from *Today in the Word,* June 29, 1992. Accessed February 27, 2013. http://www. sermonillustrations.com/a-z/p/prayer.htm.

36. Sadhu Sundar Singh quoted at Tentmaker, "Prayer and Intercession Quotes," p. 6. Accessed February 27, 2013. http://www.tentmaker. org/Quotes/prayerquotes6.htm.

37. Richard Owen Roberts quoted at Grace Quotes, "Revivial-Obstacles." Accessed February 27, 2013. http://www. thegracetabernacle.org/quotes/Revival-Obstacles.htm.

38. Leonard Ravenhill, *Why Revival Tarries* (Minneapolis: Bethany House, 1987), 25.

39. Leonard Ravenhill, *Revival God's Way: A Message to the Church* 2006 ed. (Bloomington, MN: Bethany House, 1983, 2006), 64.

40. G. Campbell Morgan quoted at OChristian.com, "Christian Quotes." Accessed February 2, 2011. http://christian-quotes. ochristian.com/G.-Campbell-Morgan-Quotes/page-2.shtml.

41. William Temple quoted at OChristian.com, "Christian Quotes." Accessed February 27, 2013. http://christian-quotes.ochristian. com/William-Temple-Quotes/.

42. Wesley Duewel, *Revival Fire* (Grand Rapids: Zondervan, 1995), 14.

Was the experience a

"Great Awakening?"...
a spiritual movement?...
the unleashing of God's power and glory?...
God's Kingdom movement?...
an experience of His Shekinah glory?...
or was it just simply a revival?

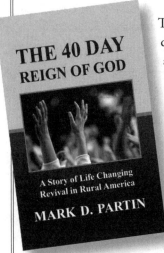

THE 40 DAY REIGN OF GOD

A Story of Life Changing Revival in Rural America

MARK D. PARTIN

The experience in question occurred during October and November of 2006, at Indiana Avenue Baptist Church. It is challenging to explain; certainly impossible to define; and not easy to describe with mere words. For some it may even be difficult to comprehend. However, for all involved it is undeniable that God opened the heavens for forty days and poured upon us immense blessings. It is undeniable that God's breath entered each of us, causing us the rise in unity as a vast army. We became His army charged with changing the world, even if only in a small way.

Prices: 1 copy: $7.99 • 2-9 copies: $6.50 each
10 or more copies: $5.00 each

There are seasons in the Christian life when we seem to grow weary and faint-hearted in the work of the Lord. Circumstances of daily living as well as the onslaughts of darkness seem to hound our every step and attempt to go forward. Setbacks have ways of interjecting discouragement and fear in our hearts and we long for freedom and rest. We find that our hands and hearts reach out for answers and long for freedom and fruitfulness. That is where the truths in the book you now hold in your hand have been written for such a time as this.

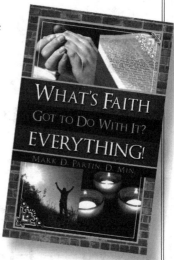

Prices: 1 copy: $7.99 • 2-9 copies: $6.50 each
10 or more copies: $5.00 each

Mark D. Partin is the director of Minister to Minister International, a ministry of prayer and revival. He has a passion for true revival in the lives of people around the world. Mark experienced continuous revival for 40 days in his church with the revival atmosphere lasting 11 months. As a result of this revival experience, he has traveled the world, teaching pastors and preaching the revival message.

"Commit these to faithful men who will teach others also." II Timothy 2:2

For more information or to contact
Mark for a Revival or Conference

Visit **www.ministertominister.org**
(423) 562-3420 or (423)562-8981
markdpartin@yahoo.com